WORKSITE MARKETING

A Promise to Deliver

Millennium Star Publishing
Chagrin Falls, Ohio

Worksite Marketing – A Promise to Deliver

Published by

Millennium Star Publishing, LLC
46 Chagrin Plaza #103
Chagrin Falls, Ohio 44022
(440-286-2010)
www.millenniumstarpublishing.com

Disclaimer
The authors and publishing company have researched all sources to ensure the accuracy and completeness of the information contained in this book. However, we assume no responsibility for errors, inaccuracies, omissions or any other inconsistency herein. Any slights against people or organizations are unintentional. Each author's chapter is the sole opinion of that author and does not reflect the opinions or business practices of the publishing company or the other authors and the companies they represent. The authors and publishing company shall have neither liability nor responsibility to any person or entity with respect to any loss or damage caused, or alleged to have been caused, directly or indirectly, by the information contained in this book. Readers should consult an attorney or accountant for legal and tax advice.

ISBN 978-0-9799807-9-4

Library of Congress Control Number: 2008921412

Cover and Typesetting by Susie Ward, The Admin Source, Inc.

ATTENTION CORPORATIONS and PROFESSIONAL ORGANIZATIONS: Quantity discounts are available on bulk purchases of this book for educational, training and gift purposes.For information contact Millennium Star Publishing, 46 Chagrin Plaza #103, Chagrin Falls, Ohio 44022; phone 440-286-2010 or msp@millenniumstarpublishing.com

Dedication

This book is dedicated to the employers who have the foresight and wisdom to offer voluntary insurance products and services to their employees; to the employees and their families who benefit from the offer and whose lives have been improved because of what we do; and to the agents, brokers, carriers, enrollers and other worksite providers who care enough to conduct their business with honesty, integrity and the sincere desire to be of service to others.

Acknowledgment

A heartfelt thank you to the generous contributing authors who so willingly agreed to condense years of experience and expertise into a handful of words. Only those well seasoned and proficient at their craft could produce such a significant result. Your desire to share your knowledge and your enthusiasm speaks volumes and I am proud to have worked with you on this exciting project.

To the staff of Millennium Star Publishing and especially to Dave for his scrolls of transcribed interviews and never-ending editing tweaks, Carmen for her virtual assistance, and Susie at The Admin Source for her transcriptions, cover design, typesetting and always-speedy guidance. To Chris, for agreeing to edit the entire manuscript during the holidays. Your innate abilities, attention to detail, work ethic and integrity leave me amazed. And to Bob for patiently listening and caring about the outcome.

Patricia J. Redic
Chagrin Falls, Ohio

Table of Contents

Introduction

What exactly is worksite marketing? It is simply a delivery system. Marketing is a way to introduce a product or service to the marketplace and worksite defines the location. Therefore, anything marketed or sold at a place of business could qualify as worksite marketing. One could worksite market chocolate-chip cookies during lunch hour in the parking lot of a manufacturing company.

Traditionally and in the insurance world, worksite marketing has meant the sale of voluntary insurance and insurance-related products and services to employees at their work location through the convenience of payroll deduction. But it is so much more than that. Worksite marketing is not only the delivery method, but also the promise to make that delivery. Unlike warm chocolate-chip cookies that can be unwrapped, sniffed and immediately enjoyed, insurance products do not offer instant gratification. We have nothing to give our buyers except a promise for future delivery in their time of need. They cannot show this promise off to their neighbors, drive it around town or wave it in their front yards. But unlike most things, our promise will never disappear. Even if we are not here to personally deliver on it, our promise persists.

This book was created to educate, encourage and promote the true meaning of worksite marketing, and to bring to light the enormous yet largely unseen impact of this industry niche. While each author explores the intricacies of his or her specialty, the common threads of sincerity and passion leap from every page.

After reading this book, you will come away with the knowledge needed to begin, rekindle or rethink your relationship with this powerful means of providing for others. If you are an agent, broker or carrier, you will learn how to improve and build upon your current practice. If you are an employer or human resource professional, you will come away with a high regard for the proficiency, professionalism and, most importantly, the heartfelt passion that these authors embody. This book, like worksite marketing, promises to deliver, and it honors that promise.

What Is It That We Really Do?

Dear Reader,

For those of us in the workplace arena, our normal activities consist of making calls to get in front of a prospect, going out and fact finding, discovering needs, putting together a proposal, closing the deal and sending in our enrollment team to take applications. We then send the data to the insurance company, get the policies issued, set up the billing and administration, collect our commissions and then go out and do it again.

Even after 22 years in the business, I still can't wait to get up in the morning to spread the word about worksite benefits to potential clients and employees. I am often reminded of just how important our work really is and the great responsibility we have to our clients. Below is just one story that brings to light the significance of what we do.

At a recent enrollment, I listened as one of my counselors talked with Lisa, a 27-year-old single mother who lived paycheck to paycheck making $12 an hour as a phone operator. She said that she and her two children shared a home with her mother, who was living on social security. As Lisa sipped a coffeehouse latté, completely disinterested in the short-term disability and term life policies we were offering, she emphatically stated, "I barely make enough money to pay for my necessities." This is a typical story and a situation we often let pass us by because there are many more potential buyers to see within the allotted enrollment time.

After Lisa signed the declination of coverage waiver, I asked her to give me just five more minutes of her time. I carefully explained that for the cost of two of those coffees, I could provide peace of mind to her and her family. I explained, "I know you love your children and that you are a hard-working mom just trying to get by. But remember, you are only a few paychecks away from being unable to pay for your necessities should an accident or sickness prevent you from working."

I also explained that should she die prematurely, the insurance company would provide the money needed to allow the grandmother to raise the children. I certainly was not trying to be negative, but was merely discussing real-life problems and real solutions. For just $12 a week she could receive a $1,200 monthly tax-free disability benefit along with a $150,000 (20-year term) policy. For one hour's pay she could buy peace of mind. Lisa, a total stranger to me a mere 15 minutes ago, had the opportunity to choose a favorable outcome for a potentially catastrophic situation.

We all have stories like this one. We often forget that, if not for us, employees would never have the opportunity to purchase the products we are selling. They would never have the chance to provide for unforeseen events that happen every day.

We should take a few moments to reflect on the individuals we sit with each day and think about the impact we will have on their lives in the future. We are selling valuable products and an important service, but what we really do is provide life-changing opportunities to people we may never see again. Yet in their darkest hour, those 15 minutes spent with us can affect the rest of their lives. That is a responsibility that should not be taken lightly.

We should take that extra step to paint a picture of what will truly happen if the client becomes disabled or dies. The extra five minutes spent with a difficult employee could make all the difference during their time of need. Remember, people don't care about how much we know until they know how much we care. Be passionate about what we do. Start today to make a difference one employee at a time. Be proud of our profession and eager to tell people, "Yes, I sell insurance."

Respectfully,

Michael D. Perna
President and Founder
Voluntary Benefits Specialists, LLC

A Word From The Top

The 2002 President of the Million Dollar Round Table has this to say...

"Worksite marketing is one of the most cost efficient tools for reaching and providing the necessary education and insurance products to Middle America. This book, *Worksite Marketing – A Promise to Deliver*, will provide you with the knowledge gleaned from successful insurance professionals and business owners to become a skilled and trusted professional advisor in the worksite market."

Marvin H. Feldman, CLU, ChFC, RFC
President and CEO of the LIFE Foundation

CHAPTER ONE

Winning At Worksite

RONALD AGYPT
SENIOR VICE PRESIDENT
COMBINED WORKSITE SOLUTIONS, AN AON COMPANY

Teamwork

Worksite marketing is a lot like baseball. There are many individuals who must come together to form a team. A successful team is always greater than the sum of its parts. Individual players working together as a cohesive entity can, and will, reach goals that would otherwise be unattainable. The challenge in worksite is to take eight different groups and shape them into an efficient unified team working toward an agreed-upon objective.

But who are the players and how do we get all of the worksite team members to work as one unit? Lest we leave anyone hopelessly confused like Costello was when Abbot attempted to identify the names of the players on a baseball team, let's meet the worksite lineup:

- The employer or owner who makes the decision to implement the worksite program
- The human resource professional who advocates and supports the worksite program
- The employee who purchases the products
- The manager of the payroll department
- The various other department managers and heads
- The carrier or multiple carriers
- The enrollment firm
- The broker or consultant who owns the relationship and case

Ensuring that each member of the team works in harmony with the other players is the key to the success of each enrollment.

The Employer

Nothing happens in worksite until the employer gives the final approval for business to move forward. The employer will usually say yes to our proposal once we have shown the added value we can offer the company. One of the best ways to prove our value is by discussing how we can positively impact employee retention. A 5-percent increase in employee retention can increase productivity from 25 percent to 65 percent[1].

The effectiveness with which a company communicates the value of its health benefits can do more to retain top-performing employees than the actual richness of the benefits themselves, according to a new analysis by Watson Wyatt. The same study also found that among employers that offer rich benefits but have poor communication strategies, the average turnover rate is 17 percent for top-performing employees. Among employers that offer less costly benefits but have effective communication strategies, the average turnover rate is 12 percent among top performers. Supplementing rich benefit programs with effective communication practices yields employers an even lower average turnover rate of only 8 percent among top performers.

Only 22 percent of surveyed employees at organizations that poorly communicate the value of their rich benefit programs are satisfied with their benefit package. Conversely, 76 percent of employees at organizations that effectively communicate the value of less-rich benefit packages are satisfied. The effectiveness of the communication of the benefits' value is clearly the determining variable and not the richness of the benefit package itself.

Another challenge faces many employers today, and that is the current trend of the aging workforce that continues to increase employer health costs. Companies that cannot hold their health-care budgets down as a share of total compensation have higher turnover rates for top performers. This is causing employers to look for solutions that allow them to cut costs and/or benefits. Voluntary benefits, when offered properly, can help a business become more productive, efficient and effective. Employers need to provide their employees with the opportunity to protect themselves and their families at the employees' own discretion and out of their own pockets.

Voluntary benefits can help respond to these and other challenges by offering greater benefit levels, ease of purchase, awareness of risk, enhanced planning, capital preservation and an improved work-life balance for employees.

The Human Resources Department

Human resources departments are typically concerned about worksite products directly competing with their core benefit program and the current employee benefits education system. Therefore, it is imperative that human resources understand how worksite products integrate with and enhance their current plans and procedures. If the human resources department does not buy into and support the worksite program, the initiative will fail.

Key issues for a human resources department involve reduction and addition. Reduction can include relieving the department's time and effort, eliminating data-collection and enrollment responsibilities, reducing administrative costs and assisting with other challenges.

Once we address potential reduction issues, we discuss enhancing employee satisfaction, morale, education and communication to help lower the client's employee turnover. It is important to understand the needs of the client's human resources managers and align coverage and services with those needs. For example, if human resources is looking to offset some of the company's current medical plan gaps, then supplemental medical, critical illness, mini med, vision care and dental care could present potential opportunities.

We must offer value to human resources and make the entire voluntary benefits experience easy for them. This is an important part of our key person discussions. I personally emphasize this point when drafting a partnership agreement with a client and provide numerous and specific examples of the value of this partnership. I stress that my worksite organization needs the full support and advocacy of the client's human resources department. That is the only way for the enrollment team to achieve its stated goals.

The Employees

It is important to look at the demographics of each employer group as well as the economic and social issues that its employees face.

Economic issues:

- Rising health care costs
- Building a retirement fund
- Protecting savings
- Challenges associated with short- and long-term disability

These factors must be considered during pre-enrollment planning and in the meetings with each employee. The worksite arena has numerous products to address these economic concerns, such as:

- Disability insurance
- Permanent life insurance
- Financial planning services
- Legal services
- Auto/homeowners insurance
- Critical illness coverage
- Medical bridge coverage
- Supplemental medical coverage
- Long-term care insurance

Social issues

- Generational differences - The product offering should assist with important events in a person's life. A young couple just getting married, buying a home, or having a child is usually interested in disability coverage, dental, vision or a permanent life insurance product. A more mature person might be interested in adding a whole life or universal life product to their portfolio. In both instances, critical illness and long-term care insurance may address additional concerns the employee may have.
- Feelings of entitlement
- Work-life balance

Considerations must be made for these and other social issues and can be addressed by suggesting:

- Medical retiree products
- Legal services
- Pet insurance
- Identity theft insurance
- Concierge services

Choosing the best products requires an in-depth analysis in advance of the enrollment, along with creative marketing tools for use during the enrollment. For example, a needs-analysis brochure helps employees choose the right benefits based on their individual needs and offset gaps in their core coverage. To build employee confidence in the worksite company, include quality products with either guaranteed or preferred underwriting that typically cost less than the equivalent of one hour's pay per week.

There are also many value-added tools that can be offered to employees during the enrollment, such as customized benefits statements and education on core benefit issues. This communication opportunity not only helps employees see their true worth to the organization, but also re-emphasizes the value of the employer's benefits offering.

The Payroll Department

The client's payroll department can make or break a worksite case. I have seen a case of more than 20,000 employees fail to go to enrollment because the payroll personnel thought it was too much work. The key to getting the payroll department to buy into the project is to make them feel they are a part of the team. Explaining the importance of their contribution can help in this process. The most important time to communicate with payroll personnel is before they receive the first bill. Continued communication during and after the initial enrollment is also important. To feel they are part of a winning team, the payroll staff must be appreciated and recognize that they are a vital part of the worksite process.

The Other Department Managers

Other valuable worksite team members are the various department heads and managers. Locally, they can make or break the case. It is critical to obtain approval from this group by showing the added value that the process can deliver to their employees. Most managers want to protect and guide their employees. Therefore, it is important to eliminate all executive skepticism by showing how the entire process works, why it will be good for employees, and how easy it is to accomplish. Once this is done, the enrollment should proceed smoothly.

The Carrier

Another important part of the worksite team is the carrier. Carriers are most interested in the proper spread of risk and the quality of business that is brought to them. Carriers look for a majority of enrolled employees, low cancellation rates and high long-term persistency. When choosing a carrier, it is important to consider product quality, service from the back room, underwriting capabilities, carrier relationships and commissions.

The Enrollment Firm

It is important to pair the right enrollment firm with the right client, employees, human resources manager, broker and carrier. Choose an enrollment firm with well-trained, professional counselors. Match unique enrollment situations with enrollment companies that offer the options and opportunities required.

The Brokers and Consultants

The manager of the case is typically a broker or consultant who provides value and trust to the client. Most brokers and consultants understand their clients and work diligently to provide value to the employer and the employees. They also act as the intermediary between all of the vendors and the client to organize a successful worksite experience.

Worksite is a relationship-driven business. The most important part of that relationship is trust, and that a deal is a deal and a promise is a promise. When a worksite case is handled appropriately, brokers or consultants can feel like their team just won the World Series.

At first glance, worksite marketing seems to be a complicated business, but it can run effectively and efficiently when the players are identified, when their roles are understood and when business is conducted properly. Winning at worksite is simple and you can hit a home run when you recognize that all partners must play as a team.

---

[1]*Harvard Business Review*, 2004.
"Communication Plays Critical Role In Improving Retention Power Of Health Benefits, Watson Wyatt Analysis Finds" segments excerpted from the PRNewswire-FirstCall article published on February 23, 2004. These findings correspond with the results of Watson Wyatt's WorkUSA® 2004 study.

As senior vice president of Combined Insurance Company of America, an Aon Company, **Ron Agypt** oversees elective benefit services for all national accounts. His responsibilities have included setting corporate strategy, operational performance, professional and management development, new products, value-added services, technical resource reporting, and national marketing relations.

Ron has 34 years of experience in the insurance industry. He has provided consulting and insurance services to organizations ranging in size from fewer than 100 to more than 200,000 employees. Having led more than 800 sales people by the age of 30, he is the youngest regional manager and vice president in the company's 89-year history.

Ron is a frequent public speaker at many local, regional and national functions related to management skills and elective benefits, and his articles have been published in numerous magazines. He serves on the board of directors and heads the marketing committee of the Better Business Bureau of Northern Illinois, and also serves on the board of directors of the Biltmore Country Club.

Ron and his wife, Kimberly, have three children, Christian, Brett and Tyler. They reside in a northwestern suburb of Chicago.

Ronald Agypt
Senior Vice President
Combined Worksite Solutions, An Aon Company
1000 Milwaukee Avenue, 6th Floor
Glenview, IL 60025
Phone: 847-953-8003
Fax: 847-953-8266
Email: ronald.agypt@combined.com
Website: www.combinedworksite.com

Chapter Two

Employers and Employees

CHARLES B. LANG
Employer
Founding President, 1st National Community Bank
Past President, Community Bankers Association of Ohio

JIM ETHIER
Employer
CEO, Bush's Beans

STEPHANIE KINGLEY
Employee
National Grocery Store Chain

LI YUNG
Employee
Midwest Manufacturing Company

PAUL CRANSTON JR.
Manager
Worldwide Fast Food Restaurant

Now that we've met the worksite team, let's begin by hearing from two of the key players - the employers and employees.

We interviewed dozens of employers and employees to explore their feelings about voluntary benefits and the worksite marketing process. While this is not meant to be an exhaustive or conclusive study, it does offer additional perspectives. Most of the employer responses were quite similar, and the employee responses matched in most cases. Therefore, in an effort to keep the chapter brief and concise, we selected these few respondents for their highly representative answers.

As an employer, what is the advantage of offering voluntary benefits to your employees?

Charles: The obvious answer is that we're providing something that the employees need. I think there's a personal inner satisfaction in knowing that we've done all we could to make something available to them. That's really important in terms of employee satisfaction. We've done something to help others who are close to us and who are working for us. They have a loyalty to us. Therefore, we have a loyalty to them.

If I offer a little better benefit than the next guy, it also helps me to retain my employees. We've got a great investment in our employees by training them to do a job. If we have a lot of turnover, we lose a lot of money in the training process. It's really important to us as employers to have our employees satisfied, happy and wanting to remain with the company so that we can take advantage of all we have invested in training them and getting them to the point where they're good, strong contributors.

Benefits are a good means of retaining employees, but not necessarily in attracting prospective employees. Younger employees in particular are interested in other things. The young employees want to know, "What am I going to get paid?" rather than, "What's going to be provided for me when I'm gone?" They think they'll live forever. They don't ask, "What's going to be there for me upon retirement?" A prospective employee might ask about those things, but it isn't a great inducement. I think the stronger portion of it is the retention of good people.

Jim: It seems to me that any time the company can use its buying power to offer our employees a benefit, then it is appropriate for us to do so. However, it is really hard to gauge to what extent our employees appreciate that opportunity.

Do you value voluntary benefits?

Stephanie: Yes, it shows that my employer cares.

Li: I appreciate it when there is no ulterior motive behind it. I don't want to see other benefits changed or lessened a few months after the voluntary benefits take effect.

Paul: Yes, as long as there is no pressure to take the benefits. I think my employer should do everything it can for its employees, especially if it doesn't cost the employer. Ideally, employees would like to see everything paid for by the employer. However, we know that isn't realistic. Voluntary benefits help to fill in the gaps the employer cannot afford to fill.

Do voluntary benefits attract you to work for a particular company? Do the benefits tie you to an employer?

Stephanie: If all things were equal, such as salary and other benefits, I would surely want to work for the company that offered more in terms of benefits, voluntary and otherwise. If the benefits could not leave with me, then I would have to factor in the value of the benefits versus the value of another job.

Li: I would be attracted to work with a company that offered the most benefits, simply because that makes a statement that the employer is interested in taking care of its employees. However, I would not stay at a bad job simply because of the benefits.

Paul: Right now I'm looking for the most salary. Perhaps as I get older, benefits will become more important to me. But for now, I need to work for the compensation in terms of money. I do have friends at the company who have some medical problems, and are staying to keep their benefits. I do feel that a company that takes the time to research and offer additional benefits to their employees is not only an attractive company to work for, but also one that cares about their employees, a key ingredient in making it a good place to stay.

As an employer, are there any downsides or risks that you encounter when making a voluntary benefit available?

Charles: Clearly, one of the big risks is the person we're doing business with. It's very important for the presenter of the product to convince the employer that he or she is going to provide a quality product, will be there to service it, has been around for a while, and will be around for a lot longer to take care of the employees' needs.

Jim: I think there are two downsides. One is that we do have to stop the production lines to explain all of this. Obviously, that would be taking time away from productive activity in other areas. The second issue has always troubled us a little bit. When we get too many deductions from the paycheck, it may in fact cloud what the employees think they're really paid.

As an employee, do you see any downsides to a voluntary benefit offering?

Stephanie: If the offer is truly voluntary, I don't see any downside. After all, I can just say no.

Li: If the offer included a lot of great benefits, I might be tempted to take them all, and that would affect my paycheck. But I guess that is a personal choice. I'd much rather have too many choices than none at all.

Paul: Only if the people presenting the offer were pushy or high pressure. But if the insurance people come in with information and are friendly and polite, I don't see any downside to it.

How do you as an employer decide what products to offer your employees?

Charles: I try to involve other people within the organization, realizing that a product that suits me may not suit another person. I would want to bring the human resources officer into the conversation because he or she is probably much closer to the employees' needs for those kinds of benefits. If I didn't have an HR person, I would bring in somebody whom I felt represented the average person, communicated well and had the respect of the other employees. I would get that person involved to help make the decision as to what products are most needed and appealing to the employees.

Jim: That decision is largely made by the folks in our HR department. They sift through all of the approaches, see something of value, and then bring it to our executive committee. For instance, the determination to offer long-term care was an education process that HR undertook to bring a better understanding among the executive committee members as to why it would be an appropriate benefit.

Should employees have a say in the product decision?

Charles: The biggest drawback to that is without a proper presentation of what the product is, the employees won't really know enough to make an intelligent decision. One of the real values of salesmanship is that people will perceive a need when the product is properly presented.

Jim: Certainly we like to consider the employee's voice, but we have to be careful that we don't have a few people who make a lot of noise versus a broad-based employee desire for a certain benefit. We conduct culture surveys, Gallup polls and those types of things.

Do you think you should have input regarding the benefits your employer offers?

Stephanie: We have several thousand employees here. It would be difficult to poll everyone. The employer and HR should know what benefits are missing from our employer-paid package and should offer those. I wouldn't want to see a duplication of benefits. Then it becomes difficult to choose one over the other. It's not easy to please everyone, so the employer has to make an educated decision as to what would be appropriate to offer. However, they should always have an ear to the employees to find out what we're saying. If the company is small, it might be appropriate to ask the employees.

Li: I think an employer should take the employee population's culture into consideration. Things such as income levels, current benefits, family conditions and situations should come into play when deciding on a benefit to offer. It may be difficult to ask every single employee, but the employer may want to have a representative task force to help with the decision.

Paul: I understand that this might be hard to do and that the answers would be all over the board. A smart employer knows what is not being covered and hopefully listens to what employees are saying throughout the year. It shouldn't be too hard to know what the employees would appreciate. However, I wouldn't mind being asked ahead of time.

As an employer, how do you want to be approached by someone who is offering voluntary benefits? What do you like and what turns you off?

Charles: Referrals are very important. If I can talk to somebody who has had a positive experience with the party offering the product, that's really important. That's probably the best way for brokers or agents to get into any company.

Telephone calls may be a way to try to get an appointment, but I don't think that very many people in my business are buying products based on what they hear in a telephone conversation. Everybody is getting the telephone sales pitches and I think they're turned off by those. With a personal call, it really helps if you can have an introduction first.

If the goal is to get your foot in the door, some form of a personal presentation is the best way to approach the employer.

Jim: I'd like to see some type of white paper that really gives me an in-depth explanation and understanding of the importance of this benefit, including what problems it addresses and what peer companies are doing.

In short, something that explains not only the benefit and how it works, but also why I should do it. I want to see something that is candid that talks about some of the downsides and pitfalls. I want to be able to sit down and deal with this with some level of objectivity.

As an employee, how do you want to be presented with a voluntary benefit offering? Who should assist with the actual enrollment?

Stephanie: I'd like to get plenty of information prior to signing up so I can read it and take it home for my husband to read. I'd like to have a knowledgeable third party assist me. I wouldn't want to enroll myself for fear of making a mistake, and I don't think that an HR department has the background to understand all of the fine points of multiple benefits. I'd like to have the time to sit one-on-one with someone who can help me understand and decide upon the best benefits for my situation.

Li: The employer should give the employees ample notice and lots of information before the sign-up day. I don't care who assists with the enrollment as long as they take the time to explain the benefits so I understand how they can help me with my particular needs. I don't want someone to try to shove a benefit at me if it doesn't make sense for me. I want everything to be simple to understand and simple to do. I would not want to sign up all by myself. I want someone to answer my questions honestly, without a sales slant.

Paul: I want someone assigned to me who takes the time to understand my personal financial situation and give me straightforward advice about the selection of benefits. I'm not sure that an HR person or employer can do this, because they are not trained in all of the benefits. I also don't think it is the HR person's business what benefits I select or why I select them. A trained insurance person should assist with the enrollment with confidentiality being important. I don't want to be rushed through the process either.

From an employer's standpoint, when it comes to voluntary benefits, what is most important to you when making a decision to do business with someone? Is it the products offered, your relationship with the person, the companies that person represents, their credentials and testimonials from others, the level of involvement required of you, or the ease of benefits administration?

Charles: It's probably a combination of some of those things. It's really important that the people who come in to talk to the employer are good salespeople. If you're able to sell the employers on the idea that this is a good product, they'll know that you'll be able to sell it to their employees as well. That's what an employer wants.

The time spent by employers on their personnel is very important. They're paying a lot of money for that. They don't want to bring somebody in who is going to keep their employees from getting the job done while he or she is selling the product. The individual salesperson certainly is the important thing.

The employer does not want his own involvement to be more than necessary. He thinks the same thing as far as the employees are concerned. He wants you to be able to get in and present well in a short period of time. That's really important to the employer.

Offering benefits at the worksite is very efficient. You come to where the employees are to talk to them. In terms of the presentation, it is convenient because it is presented to all of the employees at one time in a very professional manner. As a result, we get greater participation.

Jim: I think the credibility of the company providing the benefit is very important -- not only the agent or broker, but the insurance carrier as well. It is almost a given that the person I'm dealing with would be professional and have a good reputation.

As an employee, what is most important to you when making a decision to purchase voluntary benefits? Is it the products offered, the person making the offer, the companies that person represents, their credentials and testimonials from others, your need, or the price?

Stephanie: Certainly all of those factors come into play, but bottom line, I would purchase a benefit first if I have a need and if the benefit fills that need, and second, if the price was affordable. However, if the salesperson making the offer was pushy or if the insurance company was not reputable, then I would not purchase anything.

Li: Since the person greeting me is the first thing I see, I may or may not listen based on that first impression. It is important to me that the salesperson is educated about the benefits, answers my questions in a truthful manner, takes time with me, understands how to explain the benefits in simple layman's terms, and that the sign-up process is simple and private. Even if I needed the benefit, I would not buy from someone who was merely trying to sell me something.

Paul: All of those factors come together as one. The offer should have products I need at a price I can afford. The person making the offer to me should be highly skilled and trained and have the ability to make me understand how the benefits would work for me. The insurance carrier should be reputable and have a history of working within this market. Hopefully, my employer would have researched all of this before asking me to make a decision.

How does an employer justify allowing employees to take time away from work to visit with a benefits counselor?

Charles: That brings us back to the product and whether it's worthwhile. If, in fact, you have demonstrated to the employers that there's value in the product and they see it in terms of gaining greater employee satisfaction and higher performance on the job, they should be willing to share reasonable amounts of the employees' time to do that.

Do you appreciate it when your employer allows you time off from work to learn about and purchase voluntary benefits?

Stephanie: Of course I do. It proves that they value me and my contribution to the organization enough to allow me to make personal and financial decisions while still getting paid.

Li: Yes, it is a nice gesture that really doesn't cost them anything. We waste that kind of time in the ladies room talking about nothing.

Paul: Anything my employer does for me is great. Maybe they could pay for the benefits. But then, that wouldn't be voluntary, right?

What are some of the positive results that you have seen as an employer by offering voluntary benefits? Are there any negatives?

Charles: I have not seen negatives, only positives. We've had several situations in which employees have been able to take advantage of or utilize benefits. Part of the reward of making the program available is when we see it being used and realize that without that program, the employee would not have had the ability to cope with a situation. The company certainly could not have afforded to spend corporate profits to provide that.

Another benefit would be the fact that it's an expression to the employees that the employer really does care about them. Although we're with the employees all the time and sometimes just assume that they know we care and are concerned, like anything else, it needs reinforcement. This reinforces that we really care about them off the job as well as on the job.

Chapter Three

Get Ready, Get Set, Enroll

TONY ROBERTS
A. Roberts & Associates, Inc.

When prospecting for voluntary benefits, getting past the gatekeeper and to the decision-maker is not always an easy task. Cold calls, walk-ins or e-mails are shotgun approaches. All we can hope is that we're contacting these folks on a day when a certain pain exists and they realize the need for our services. There's a lot of time, money, energy and effort spent on that type of introduction and it's not very efficient.

If I walk through the door to the HR department without the directive coming from higher ups, I usually hear, "This is just another task we have to deal with. We're already overworked and don't know how to get this done. Why do we want to take on another project? We'll have to run this up the ladder." For the most part, HR departments are overworked, understaffed, maybe underpaid and not considered a profit center by corporations. Why in the world would the HR director make a decision to increase the department's workload? But when the CEO or president makes the decision, the HR department becomes an implementation force. That's why I find it best to start at the top.

Three to Enroll

When the networking is in place, there's no worry about getting past the gatekeeper or the HR staff. I build relationships with the CEOs and presidents of the companies I'm trying to help. Our property and casualty agency has an affiliation with the Presidents Association. This is a group of presidents and CEOs of companies in manufacturing and other similar industries. Through this affiliation, I have permission to contact them. By using my existing relationships, I'm ready to begin the process of closing new worksite cases. I usually plan for three meetings to secure the average case and get to the point of scheduling the enrollment.

First Interview – Value, Open Arms and the HR Department

The initial meeting is with the president or CEO and the HR director or vice president of human resources. I'm breaking the ice and explaining who we are, how we can help and what we can bring to the table. When I get upper management to say, "These programs are something we want and support. Make it happen," the ball is then handed off to the HR director. When working with the HR folks I like to point out, "We want to be an extension of your human resources department. We want to bring bodies, technology and assistance to you. We're not just bringing another burden to you. We're bringing manpower to help you complete these tasks."

Our goal is to accomplish something that is usually a chore for the HR department. When it comes to enrollments, re-enrollments and introducing additional products, we do more than just come in, write a few policies, and eventually inform payroll what the premium is going to be. We relieve the HR department of a huge burden and become part of their organization. They say, "This firm is going to be able to help us with core enrollments. They will help us overcome our staff shortage." They see the value that we're adding.

When we become a problem-solver for the HR department, they support us. If we just walk in and say, "How about offering this critical illness product to your employees," we're just another vendor with another bad approach. That is why we work to build a strong relationship with added value. When we preach this sermon, the human resources department opens its arms and welcomes us to the team.

Second Interview – Products, Presentations and Heroes

During the second interview we seek specific product and service solutions to aid the corporation. We start by asking questions. Is the company growing? What benefits does the company currently offer? Which of those benefits are paid for on behalf of the employees? We talk to the client to find out what makes the best sense for them.

When we determine which product does make the most sense, I select the carrier that has the best product in that discipline. As a result, I don't have to worry about someone walking in the door behind me and asking the employer, "If these guys know what they're doing, why did they give you an inferior product?"

This speaks to the carriers we represent. I know that certain carriers have a better life product than others. I also know that they have the ability, depending on the size of the group, to give us guaranteed-issue limits and other important concessions. So we work on behalf of the client to get the products that make sense and offer easy underwriting and enrollment. As we examine what coverage is already in place, we may find shortcomings. It might be with disability, critical illness or life insurance. We then start looking for products that can fill those gaps.

For example, let's say the company recently raised the deductibles for its major medical plan. Now the employees must pay $1,000 for prescription drugs before the company kicks in and pays 20 percent. In this case, it may be important to offer a solution that gives prescription drug coverage from dollar one that the employee can buy for $14 or $15 a month.

As professionals, we have to be prepared for all kinds of situations. The more information we have about the employer, the demographics of their employees, what's going on with their current benefits, what's happened in the last few years, where they want to go and if they're growing or not, the more we can put into the presentation we're designing.

Presentation – It's About Technology

The employer presentation is key. We like to have hard-copy documentation that supports our presentation. I'm a big proponent of PowerPoint® and other technology such as overhead projectors, laptops and flipcharts. We don't hold anything back because today it's so easy to utilize technology. If we're not using it, I guarantee that our competitor is. Our competition has access to the same carriers and the same products as we do. So it's not about the products, it's about the process we're wrapping around the products that's going to either get us the case or not.

Currently, we're working with a multi-thousand-person group. We spent $10,000 to build a website that was part of our presentation. We wanted to show how committed we were to obtaining the client. We also wanted them to see that once they gave us the green light, we were ready to go. Their employees could automatically go to this website and learn about what we're offering. It's all about taking the time to educate and communicate.

Presentation – It's About Time

Some employers say, "Look, we don't want our people to take time off the floor." We let them know that the employee presentation will take between five and 20 minutes per person. If we make a longer presentation, we are going to lose them. After about five minutes we have a pulse on the employee. Either the employee says, "I want to know more," or "I don't want it" and they're up, out and gone.

If we're making the offer alongside a core benefit enrollment, the employer already recognizes that employee time is needed to gather the data for the HR department to forward to the proper channels. If HR is understaffed and overworked, re-enrollment is a huge stress for them and our skilled enrollment team can alleviate some of the burden. When appropriate, I remind the employer that many of the voluntary products are eligible for Section 125 and that for every dollar sheltered, a tax savings comes back to the employer. So the short amount of time we spend with each employee can save the employer in the long run.

In my experience, a benefit offering of three or more products is offering too much. I like to offer one benefit. We get a better enrollment because we don't confuse the employees. Larger companies may want to offer two pieces, but anything beyond that is confusing to the audience and causes them to lose focus. On the high end, there may be $35 to $45 a month that an employee can contribute toward supplemental products for a family. If we go in there and try to knock somebody's head off at $80 a month, all we're going to do is cause heartache. The policy will most likely lapse and nobody wins. Supplemental products need to be affordable and, in the case of a claim, they need to bring dollars back to the client in an amount that far exceeds the premium paid.

We value repeat business, long-term relationships and referrals. So when we tell the employer, "You don't have to get that involved in the process," we make sure that we work with carriers that are capable of backing us up. We must be certain that our product providers have the ability to and history of producing proper bills and timely premium credits. When we tout a seamless venture, we must produce. We can be the greatest salespeople in the world, but if the support is not there on the back end, we'll have problems.

Presentation - It's About Caring

I tell my employer clients, "For the most part, your workforce life insurance needs are taken care of by your group life insurance. However, when employees terminate their employment with you, chances are good that they will lose that life insurance. If something happens to them, they're not going to have the coverage." Our $3, $5 or $10-per-week life insurance, cancer, accident or disability worksite policies may be an employee's only opportunity to participate in benefits that can truly help them and their family. We're bringing a great service and benefit to them. The employer needs to feel good about that.

The employer can get a lot of mileage out of offering guaranteed-issue insurance benefits that employees may or may not otherwise be able to obtain. If the company has a heart attack or cancer survivor who comes back to work, that employee is not eligible to get life insurance or other benefits on his or her own. But when the employer offers those employees $150,000 of guaranteed-issue life insurance, the company becomes the hero. It says a lot about an organization when it thinks enough of its employees to give them an opportunity like this.

Third Interview – Time, Dates and Action

At the third meeting with the employer, we bring back a plan of action, get signoffs and determine the dates of the enrollment. I like to work backwards with a timeline.

Let's talk about larger groups of 1,000 and up. Typically, groups of this size have effective dates of January 1 for core benefits. They tend to prefer open enrollments in October and November in order to have everything wrapped up by Thanksgiving. This gives them the last week in November and the first two or three weeks in December to get all of the data into the system so the January payroll is ready to calculate and move forward.

If we're aiming for a November 1 enrollment date, we need about 60 to 90 days of advance notice so that we have time to put all the necessary systems in place from an enrollment standpoint. We have to organize and educate our enrollment teams, communicate with the carriers and upload the software with the employer's data feeds.

This timeline also gives us the opportunity to get marketing materials out to the employees in order to introduce them to the new benefits and build the hype and excitement. This means that October, September and part of August are spent building and rolling out the marketing pieces. The decision to put these benefits in place probably took place some time in June or July. The initial meetings most likely started in the spring. So for large groups, it takes about nine months from start to finish, with not much time to spare.

Wishes, Partners and Hot Buttons

On occasion we have to honor other enrollment requests. Sometimes, in order to win the enrollment or offer new benefits, we have to supply the technology or build the enrollment platform that can support the company's core enrollment for major medical and other group products. If we're not building the platforms and the core benefit enrollment ourselves, we have to have relationships with folks who can do that for us efficiently and correctly.

A few years ago, we called on a large group in Tennessee. We had relationships with the CEO, the president and the director of HR. On our initial fact-finding mission, I looked at the HR director and asked, "If you had a wish list, tell me the top three things you would want." Aside from a new car and a fabulous vacation, she said, "We would like to produce some kind of benefits statements. Our people don't realize how much their benefits are worth."

Because of the relationships I have through worksite marketing and networking, I was able to contact a capable vendor who I knew could handle this job. We introduced the vendor to the client, created an enrollment strategy and today, that multi-thousand-group corporation is still using those benefits statements. We didn't offer any products at that time. We just brought benefits statements in order to give employees an understanding of how much the company was spending on their benefits. This enrollment would not have happened if I hadn't asked, "What's your hot button? What do you need from us? Let us see if we can do it or not." We took the HR director's wish and went forward. We put together a team to create a long-term solution. I believe that a little piece of something is better than 100 percent of nothing. Never be afraid to go out and put partnerships together that make sense. If nobody gets greedy, worksite marketing can be beneficial for all parties.

A Winning Outcome

The whole point of worksite marketing is to create win-win situations for the client, for ourselves and for everyone else involved. Let's go back to the beginning to see how this happens.

We started the process with a relationship with the president or CEO who approves the event. We then tried to overcome any objections as we earned the trust of the HR director. Our goal is to add measurable value to the HR department as we become an extension of their staff. We seek products and services based on the needs of the organization and implement the enrollment by partnering with high-quality carriers and service providers.

But ultimately, it's not just the products or process that's important. It's about the outcome. We've been given a great opportunity. We have the ability to make a difference in people's lives; people not usually solicited by the insurance community. Before each enrollment I tell my staff, "Always remember who your audience is. Be straight up with them. Be fair and honest. Don't try to overload them. Be proud of what you're offering. Know that you're bringing value, added abilities and benefits to the employer and to each and every employee you meet. Remember that what you do makes a difference."

Tony Roberts began his insurance career soon after graduation from the University of Kentucky, where he majored in mathematics. In 1985, he joined forces with a broker in Louisville, Kentucky, and in 1987 began a four-year term with F&G Life. In 1991, Tony went out on his own with a concentration on worksite and employee benefits. He continues to work in the benefits field and in 2004 added an Allstate Property and Casualty shop to his business.

With more than 20 years of worksite marketing experience, Tony understands how to reach the decision makers and create successful and profitable outcomes for all concerned.

Tony Roberts
A. Roberts & Associates, Inc.
13819 English Villa Drive
Louisville, KY 40245
Phone: 502-548-3065
Fax: 502-244-0420
Email: troberts@arobertsassociates.com
Website: www.Allstate.com/tonyroberts

Chapter Four

The Importance of Product Selection

MICHAEL D. PERNA
President and Founder
Voluntary Benefits Specialists, LLC

In workplace marketing, there are two hoops to jump through before the opportunity will arise to make the employee presentation and sale. The first hoop is the sale to the decision-makers. Are they interested in voluntary benefits? Can you help them see the value? The next hoop is to get the right working conditions and access to the employee group.

Once this is accomplished, the ultimate sale to the employee will generate a commission to pay for all the effort leading up to this event. This is why product selection is so important. The products must be the right fit for the client. After all, if the employee does not make a purchase, all of the time and energy leading up to this point go unrewarded and worse yet, uncompensated. In fact, anything less than 60 percent participation is simply trading commissions for enrollment costs. There is a direct correlation between great participation and proper product selection. An employee only has so much discretionary income to commit to voluntary products and frequently, money is spent on unnecessary products. This is not a one-size-fits-all business. Make sure to offer the right product fit along with the best pricing and underwriting.

Who Decides?

When it comes to product selection, there are two schools of thought. The first is to offer the entire portfolio of products. Since the employees are spending their own money, let them decide what is best. This reasoning is equal to no product selection at all. The second school of thought is to do the proper fact-finding first. This is the only way to understand the deficiencies in the current benefit program. After an analysis of occupations, industry, gender, ages and salary ranges, you can determine which products best complement the existing benefit package.

In my initial employer presentations, I say, "If anyone around the table has a greater knowledge of the correct product selection than I do, then fire me and hire that person." The employer or company decision-maker may be a great accountant, doctor or machine operator, but that does not make him or her an expert on insurance.

Product Selection Process

During the initial interview, ask questions about the organization. You will be better able to evaluate needs and determine an enrollment's potential profitability when you understand the company, the industry and the culture of the organization. Be sure to gather the following:

Company Information

- Name of organization
- Decision maker
- Number of eligible employees
- Number of part-time employees
- Number of employees per location
- Male-to-female ratio
- Division of employees (management, administrative, laborers, sales, etc.)
- Salaries
- Non-English speaking population

Once you have a basic understanding of the organization, learn about the current benefit package offering to see if there is a need for additional products.

Benefits Information

- Current company-paid/core benefits, such as medical, dental, vision, life (how much), short-term disability and long-term disability

- Any other company provided benefits
- Any voluntary benefits, such as life, disability, accident, cancer, critical illness, computer programs, limited medical, etc.
- Current participation in voluntary benefits

Even though the employer may be offering voluntary benefits, it is always important to learn the participation level. Often, participation is weak and the wrong products are being offered. This situation can open the door for you, allowing you to suggest additional and more suitable products.

Keep the initial interview to about 30 to 45 minutes. Only ask what you need to know. Learn about the decision-makers' experience with voluntary products--their successes, problems and what they would like to see happen in the future. At this point, ask, "If I can show you a better overall voluntary benefit package for your employees or a program that can help fill the gaps in your current program, would you be willing to move forward if my recommendations make sense to your organization?" Keep in mind that it makes no sense to go forward if this is just a courtesy appointment.

Also, find out how past enrollments have been conducted and what format has been the most successful: one-on-one, group, call center or online. If it seems to be a viable account, tell the decision-makers that you will evaluate the information and come back with recommendations. If it is a large group (500 or more employees), ask for the pertinent census information needed to prepare the formal proposal. This is the close. By allowing you to come back with recommendations, the company is showing an interest in moving forward.

Thoughts on Product Selection

- The product selection can be a joint decision process with the originating broker and/or with the client.
- Smaller cases typically accept the broker's recommendations even though the client has the final say.
- After a thorough fact-finding, the gaps in coverage should be obvious.
- Go to the marketplace to satisfy the needs of the client and to select the best product with the best underwriting at the most competitive price.

- Depending on the product(s) needed and your experience with carriers, finding the right product(s) is the easy part of the job.
- A typical breakdown of products could be short-term disability and a choice of term insurance for the least compensated employees, and universal life for the more highly paid, salaried employees, along with a cancer or critical illness policy.
- To avoid confusing employees and hurting participation, while still filling in the gaps in coverage, limit the selection to three choices.
- Keep the audience in mind, along with the average employee's amount of discretionary income.
- Favorable underwriting (few or no medical questions) is tied to participation. For smaller cases, limit the product selection to one carrier in order to satisfy participation requirements. There is more leeway in the 500-plus market. Two different carriers can be used to obtain a better choice of products and underwriting while satisfying both carriers' participation guidelines.

Presenting Products to the Employer

The audience of decision-makers typically determines the sophistication of the final presentation. In the smaller case market, the owner, office manager or benefits person typically makes the decision. It is usually a cut-to-the-chase process: What are the needs? What products satisfy the needs? Are the products competitively priced? The larger case market (500-plus) involves two or three follow-up visits. Everyone from the benefits director to the benefits manager to the CFO is involved in the process. Therefore, the presentation may need a sophisticated touch, even though it always comes down to need.

Presenting Products to the Employees

When presenting to employees, it is essential to know the audience. Every employee should have the need for the products being offered. For example, if there is no company-paid disability coverage being offered, present a voluntary payroll-deduction disability benefit. If the employer is only offering a $10,000 company-paid life policy, offer additional term or universal life. If an employee has a spouse or dependent children, convince that employee of the need for additional life insurance. Since one-on-one time is usually limited to 15 minutes, knowing which products fill that gap and being able to present those choices convincingly is essential.

Ensure that you and your enrollers are properly trained and that everyone involved fully understands the products being offered. Take the time to read the policies so that you are aware of what each one does and does not cover. Take continuing-education seminars and courses. If there is something you do not understand, ask the carrier and get all of your questions answered prior to presenting the product. Take a look at the claim forms your clients are receiving from the carriers so that you fully understand the claims-paying process. Not knowing something is not an excuse for providing wrong information. It is your job to be the expert! Ask yourself the question, "Would I buy this policy if I were the one being sold to? Is this the best carrier and best product available for the employee I am speaking to? Did I help that employee make the right product decision?" Too often, agents go through the motions of the enrollment process without really thinking about the impact they have on an employee's product decision.

Bottom Line

It is of utmost importance to choose the right product at the best price with the most favorable underwriting to fill the void in an employer's current benefit program. When you do the right job up front with thorough fact-finding, each product choice makes sense. If, on the other hand, you are just randomly throwing products at an employee, selling becomes a real chore. Keep it simple, keep it real and keep it honest. The 15 minutes you spend with total strangers should make a real difference in their lives when the time comes to use the product they purchased from you. So always keep in mind what it is that you really do for the people you encounter every day.

Michael Perna founded Perna and Associates in 1984 in New Jersey. The agency sold auto, homeowners and individual insurance policies for Prudential Insurance Company. In 1990, Michael expanded into worksite and, along with three partners, founded a new company, Custom Benefit Programs. From 1990 to 1994, he served as CEO. Michael enrolled many casinos in Atlantic City and Mississippi before moving to Las Vegas in 1994 to start his second enrollment company, Employee Benefit Communicators (EBC, INC). Serving as president from 1994 to 2006, he enrolled many high-profile accounts including Wyndham Hotels, Hard Rock Hotel, Cummins Atlantic, TGI Friday's, Krispy Kreme and Hollister Inc. In 2007, Michael made a commitment to travel less and founded Voluntary Benefits Specialists, LLC (VBS, LLC) to develop the local Las Vegas market.

Michael D. Perna
President and Founder
Voluntary Benefits Specialists, LLC
8766 S Maryland Parkway, Suite 105
Las Vegas, NV 89123
Phone: 702-533-4232
Fax: 702-837-5530
Email: MDP702@aol.com

CHAPTER FIVE

The Carriers' Perspective

CHARLES C. BAGGS, FLMI, ACS
EXECUTIVE VICE PRESIDENT AND CHIEF ADMINISTRATIVE OFFICER
ALLSTATE WORKPLACE DIVISION

An insurance carrier's job is to offer products that are valuable to employers and employees. How this is accomplished depends on the carrier's distribution system.

Most worksite carriers fall under one of three basic distribution models: integrated, partnered and shared.

Integrated - The integrated carrier is involved in the entire process, from product development to marketing, sales, new business and customer service. Because this is a career agent system, the selling agents are captive to a single carrier.

Partnered - The partnered carrier typically manufactures products, provides administrative and customer service, and works with independent agents to bring products to the market. Agents sell the business to employers and the enrollment to the consumers, or they work with an enrollment firm to conduct the enrollment. It's a joint partnership between the carrier and the independent agent.

Shared - The shared model consists of group insurance carriers that enroll group benefits first, then return to introduce and sell traditional worksite products. In this way, they leverage their existing company resources and relationships. They are typically involved in product development and, to a lesser degree, in sales, technology and customer service.

As a partnered-model worksite carrier, we work primarily with independent agents. We provide the products and services and the agents/brokers provide the opportunities and conduct the enrollment. The independent agents bring quality, diversity and professionalism to the market.

The Independent Agent/Partner Relationship

Under the partnered model, independent agents enjoy:

- The entrepreneurial opportunity to build and grow their own business
- The opportunity to select the carrier or carriers they feel are best suited to each unique enrollment. This is not necessarily the case with the integrated and shared models. Especially in the integrated model, agents are essentially employees of the carrier.
- The ability to choose to do business with a specific carrier. Many independent agents choose to work with a partnered carrier because the carrier has to put more effort into earning the agent's business every day.
- The ability to maintain control of the sales and enrollment processes. The partnered carrier assumes that the agent or broker has all of the communication, organization and sales skills needed to gain access to employees, present the products accurately, and conduct an enrollment effectively and efficiently. The integrated carrier, on the other hand, usually controls the process from beginning to end.
- Flexible training schedules. Independent agents have different schedules. The carriers cannot dictate the terms of training, so they try to make education available through Web-cast training, seminars and, if appropriate, regional field staff who assist with licensing and contracting, product knowledge training and sales process training. It is somewhat easier to hold formal training sessions with the career type agents. The carrier can say, "The agents in this geographic region are going to meet in this particular city for a training day."

No matter which model is chosen, an agent, broker, employer or HR administrator should look for and ask about a carrier's proficiency in these six key areas:

1. Commitment
2. Technology
3. Underwriting
4. Claims
5. Service
6. Compensation

Commitment

The carrier should be financially strong, committed to the worksite market, and have a primary focus on products and services that are geared toward the worksite. A carrier should understand the market and know the types of products, services and systems that are required. As in any business, the carrier must have strong values and must honor its commitments. The carrier should also have a long history of working relationships with the agents.

Technology

With technology becoming increasingly important, a carrier should utilize as much technology as reasonably possible, so long as it makes it easier for agents and brokers, as well as employers and employees, to do business.

Today, when agents sell an account, not only do they need product and service knowledge, they also have to understand and offer the technology capabilities that support the entire sales process. The goal of technology is to facilitate ease of enrolling, billing and collecting.

- **Enrollment technology**

  Paper applications yield the highest percentage of incomplete applications. As a result, agents spend a lot more time chasing missing information or underwriting requirements, which slows down the process. Technology simplifies life and makes it easier for agents by reducing the amount of follow-up they have to do.

  There are several different ways to conduct an electronic enrollment. The simple application-taker is an electronic function performed on a laptop that allows agents to enroll applications. With a good system, agents enjoy a straight-through back-end process with some automated underwriting capabilities. A substantial portion of applications can be issued without any human touches. When an application comes in via this process, it can proceed to automated underwriting and be issued on the same day.

  There are other types of electronic enrollment opportunities. Popular among employers, the core benefit enrollment system allows agents to offer employers other benefits such as major medical, 401(k)s, vision or other products not necessarily offered by the carrier. Everything is enrolled through this single system and uploaded to the various carriers.

Many independent agents use the electronic enrollment system in a call center with voice-stamping, PIN signatures and the like. Many large employers like to do online self-service enrollments, although those typically are done with group products that are easier to enroll than individually underwritten products.

- **Billing Technology**

  Billing may be the most challenging aspect of the worksite business. The employer or HR administrator does not have a lot of time to spend with a difficult billing process. When deductions are set up quickly and correctly, everything else follows. Billing and collection becomes easier, as does customer service and claims. The carrier sends the complete deduction file to the employer and e-mails the monthly bills. The employer makes the deductions and sends back an electronic file with any updates or terminations.

  People are used to doing e-business and e-exchange. If the carrier can set up an automated self-bill or electronic bill that minimizes the effort expended by the HR or accounting department to process and pay that bill, then everyone wins.

Underwriting

A worksite carrier should have a simple and smooth underwriting process that doesn't require a lot of follow-up. Agents, brokers and enrollment firms cannot spend time trying to chase medical requirements and physician statements. Underwriting has to be quick, with either simplified or a "contingent-guarantee" issue. For that reason, products should be designed to "accept or reject" based on a few questions. In the worksite market, carriers have to make swift decisions about issuing or denying coverage.

Carriers also have to ensure a good spread of risk, although they may make some underwriting exceptions within reason. In some cases, carriers may have a bit more flexibility in terms of what they will do outside of their standard underwriting offer. The first line will be underwriting the product according to the underwriting guidelines used when developing the product. Then, carriers may look at the case and ask, "What types of occupations are involved with that particular group? Will we have the right spread of risk?" They may also look at the broker and enrollment firm and ask, "Do we know the enrollment firm and will they give us good penetration so we won't be selected against?" All of these questions come into play when considering underwriting.

If agents present the right business case with the right information, a carrier will take all of that into consideration and may be able to be a little more flexible with the underwriting.

Claims

Everyone from the agent or broker to the carrier has made this promise to the employer and employees: "If you pay us premiums, we'll pay you benefits promptly at the time of a covered event." A carrier must be able to deliver on that promise at claim time. And it must be done as accurately, quickly and with as much compassion as possible so that employees can really see the benefit of having the worksite products.

Agents, enrollment firms and carriers must ensure that everything they do is in compliance with HIPAA guidelines. As a carrier, we help agents comply with HIPAA requirements by offering employees direct access to their claims information through self-service Web sites.

Another valuable service is an automated-calling process used to notify claimants of received paperwork. The policyholder receives an automated call that says, "We've received your claim. It's in progress. Typically, it takes three to four days to be processed." Then we follow up when the claim has been processed or if the claimant needs any additional information. We've also automated the processing of our wellness claims. About 93 percent of those claims are processed without examiner intervention.

Service

Policyholder service is usually a direct relationship between the carrier and the employee, although some agencies like to be involved in order to bring added value to the case. This is an additional expense agents must bear, so they have to decide if it's worth the time and effort. Carriers should be willing to do whatever an agency prefers.

The key, from a carrier standpoint, is to be able to provide flexible support to agents and their customers so that service can be as hassle-free as possible. It comes back to establishing a real partnership and a working relationship between carriers, agents and clients and earning an agent's business every day.

Compensation

Agent compensation varies by business model. As you might expect, independent agents working in the partnered environment generally earn a higher commission than agents working in the integrated or shared environment, because they contribute more to the sale.

Aside from sales commissions, there are other factors agents should consider when evaluating the complete compensation package:

- **Account ownership -** Do the accounts an agent brings to the carrier belong to the carrier or the agent?
- **Vesting -** Are commissions paid fully vested at the onset of the relationship, or do commissions vest on a scale? If they vest on a scale, how long does it take for commissions to become fully vested?
- **Frequency** - How often are commissions paid and how quickly are they paid after the sale? Are advances paid on written business?
- **Promotional and incentive support** - Are agents recognized and rewarded for superior results? What is the value of the incentives and how often are they awarded?
- **Bonuses -** Are agents recognized and rewarded for superior enrollment penetration and persistency performance?

Roles, Responsibilities and Relationships

Just like carriers, agents and brokers have different operating models and diverse ways of conducting worksite business. So, when working with independent agents, carriers must be flexible enough to accommodate and support multiple enrollment processes, and provide the necessary tools, from technology and communication, to collateral, custom brochures and streaming videos. Regardless of the agent's preferred method of operation, it is the responsibility of the carrier and the agent to create a successful enrollment outcome for the employer and employees.

At the end of the day, a carrier has two major assets. The obvious one is capital, or the policyholders' premiums. Carriers must wisely invest those monies and be good stewards of them so that when claim time arrives, the benefits will be paid. The second most important asset is the carrier's people. An ideal agent or broker is somebody we can partner with to bring value to the employer and employees. And like any partnership, each party has different roles that must be understood from the very beginning.

Once we have processed applications, initiated deductions, issued policies and reconciled premiums, we simply need to deliver on our promise. That's the carrier's final responsibility.

Charles Baggs earned his master's degree in business administration from the University of Georgia. In 1985, he joined American Heritage Life and in 1990 was promoted to senior vice president of administration and technology. Charles continued in this role after the 1999 acquisition of American Heritage Life by the Allstate Corporation. The marketing name for American Heritage Life was changed to Allstate Workplace Division and in 2002, Charles was named executive vice president and chief administrative officer. With his leadership, Allstate Workplace Division has leveraged technology, including a comprehensive electronic-enrollment strategy, to make it easier to do business with Allstate Workplace Division.

Charles is responsible for all aspects of Allstate Workplace Division's operations, technology and home-office support, and develops and executes strategic plans to ensure that operations and technology support the company's objectives and satisfy producer, client and policyholder needs. He is the lead Champion of Six Sigma initiatives at Allstate Workplace Division. Charles is a member of the board of directors for American Heritage Life Insurance Company, a wholly owned subsidiary of the Allstate Corporation. He is president of Concord Heritage Life, and a member of the board of directors for Concord Heritage Life Insurance Company and First Colonial Insurance Company, wholly owned subsidiaries of American Heritage Life Insurance Company.

Charles currently serves on the Business Advisory Council for the University of North Florida and is on the board of directors for Baptist Medical Center in Jacksonville, Florida. He has also served on the boards of the Alliance for Education in Jacksonville, Florida, and the Multiple Sclerosis Society. Charles and his wife, Claudia, reside in Jacksonville, Florida.

Charles C. Baggs, FLMI, ACS
Executive Vice President and Chief Administrative Officer
Allstate Workplace Division
1776 American Heritage Life Drive
Jacksonville, FL 32224
Phone: 904-992-2613
Fax: 904-992-2939
Email: cbaggs@allstate.com
Website: www.allstateatwork.com

CHAPTER SIX

Life Matters

ROBERT H. NOE
CEO
MILLENNIUM BENEFITS GROUP

From the Board Room to the Break Room

Why would an agent go from the board room, where he was selling multi-million-dollar life insurance contracts to the break room, where he was offering $5 weekly premiums? Why would someone leave his backyard and travel the entire country, incurring more expenses and spending more time coordinating enrollments and enrollers, juggling carriers and product options?

My belief in the power of life insurance compelled me to reach out to a wider audience. Worksite marketing offered a way to impact more people, more families. After 25 years of financial planning, estate planning, buy-and-sell agreements and agent captivity, I guess it didn't make sense to the outside world to change my direction so drastically. "You'll never make it in worksite. You've been talking to the movers and shakers for all of these years; people with money to spare, with money to invest. Middle America lives from paycheck to paycheck. They spend their money on necessities, not insurance. They're a hard sell."

These were the words I heard from more than several associates as I closed my first worksite case more than 15 years ago. Yes, going from the board room to the break room was a big change, but it has proven to be a rewarding decision. Paying a $15,000 or $50,000 death claim is no less important than paying a $2-million or $5-million death claim. The money means as much to one family as it does to the other. Everyone's life and death matters to someone else. The need to provide for one's family and loved ones is universal.

Building a Business

The board room side of life insurance only allows for a few large sales and policies per year compared with the thousands that are issued via worksite marketing. After years of training as a captive agent, it was only natural to transfer the same large case business mentality to my worksite company. Our office protocols and processes remain the same. We treat each and every worksite client, both the employer and all of the participating employees, as elite and individual customers. Every client has a file with copies of their applications, as well as any correspondence and service changes. Our staff takes all of the service phone calls and responds to each request with as much care and time as we formerly spent with our boardroom clients. Worksite marketing is a business and should be set up and treated like a business. Therefore it's not only important to know the products and how they work, but it is crucial to know the clients and what they need, what they have and what they want. Building a business in worksite marketing is about intertwining people, products, processes and passion to create successful solutions for everyone.

Creating Successful Solutions

When considering suitable products to complement existing benefits plans, look for:

1. The Reality: Pay attention to the current statistics. What do industry studies show when it comes to the numbers affected by cancer, for example or the financial outcomes of these occurrences. Offer benefits that address the most likely occurrences.

2. The Impact: Look at the potential payout for the dollars spent. What benefits offer the most "bang for the buck"? Avoid trading dollars. A plan that costs $5 per week or $260 per year that is only worth $260 in services or benefits does not make practical use of premium money. However, that same $5 per week can buy thousands of dollars worth of life insurance coverage.

It's important to look at the value of a product in terms of its utilization:

a. Reality – Everyone will die, but will everyone need ...?
b. Impact – Which will affect a family the most: premiums spent for ... or premiums spent to protect a breadwinner's income?

Life insurance meets these criteria

- Statistics prove that 100 percent of the population will die
- Life insurance has a high payout for the dollar spent
- Life insurance satisfies the reality and impact questions

Life insurance is the easiest benefit to explain and understand. Therefore, it takes less time to enroll, which is something most employers appreciate. It is also the easiest benefit to administer because of the low frequency of utilization: once in a lifetime per person. Human resources administrators seldom have to deal with claim forms and the problems associated with employee's questions regarding coverage details. Most importantly, if maintained, life insurance has the highest (100-percent) eventual utilization. When building a plan based on what is most important and what will most likely happen to the most people, life insurance rises to the top. This is not to negate the importance of any other benefit possibility, but simply to make a case for the wise use of what little discretionary funds most employees have to spend on a weekly basis.

Types of Life Insurance

Life insurance can be broken down into two types of policies: term insurance and permanent insurance. Term coverage allows for the purchase of pure death-benefit coverage at inexpensive rates that are scheduled to increase with time. Permanent coverage such as whole life and universal life provide for level premiums and the tax-deferred accumulation of cash.

Term:

- Term insurance, by design, offers a temporary solution to a permanent problem.
- Term insurance rates always increase. When offered on a payroll-deducted basis, this means more work for the payroll department, as rates continually need to be changed. Eventually, many employees tire of the increases and cancel the coverage.
- If policies are not issued on a timely basis, for whatever reasons, employees may experience an unwelcome rate change prior to the first deduction because of a change of age.

- With term insurance, if an employee misses a deduction or two because of layoff, leave, etc., the policy will lapse. Partial payments are as good as no payments.

Whole Life:

- Whole-life policies are filled with rate and cash-value guarantees that satisfy the concerns "Will it be there when I need it?" and "Will the premiums stay the same?"
- Whole-life insurance also demands that premiums are paid in full and on a timely basis. If a premium is missed or the payment is late, the policy will lapse. Once again, partial payments are worthless.

Universal Life:

- Universal life is a more forgiving policy by design and therefore more suited to the variables associated with worksite marketing. Extra premiums can be dumped into the policy to beef up the cash value. If an occasional premium is missed or is late, as is quite common, the policy will use its own available internal cash value to make up the deficit.
- Because a universal-life policy is flexible, it is vital to run some illustrations prior to offering the product. To satisfy the "Will it be there when I need it?" concern, ensure that the suggested premiums or target premiums are enough to sustain the coverage. Don't take the carrier's sales representative's word for it. Check it yourself. Make sure that the premiums allow the policy to survive at the guaranteed interest rate. Run the illustration to age 100 and use the premiums that satisfy that at the guaranteed interest rate. No one wants the policy to crash and burn when the employee reaches age 65 or 70.

Reasons to Offer Permanent Life Insurance:

- Most families do not have adequate life insurance protection.
- More than half of all employees only have their company-sponsored group term life insurance coverage. They have no additional permanent protection beyond this coverage.
- At retirement, almost all employees lose their group term life coverage. That is why statistics show that less than two percent of

all death benefits paid come from a group plan. These plans give employees a false sense of security that comes to a screeching halt when they retire or quit work. Left with no coverage, they may be too old or too sick to afford the premiums of a new policy.

- The good news is that most if not all voluntary plans are portable upon retirement or termination, meaning that employees can buy a quality plan at the worksite and keep it until it is needed.

A Differentiating Factor

If the case qualifies, leave the competition behind by offering a guaranteed-issue life insurance product. Unlike most plans in the marketplace, this simple non-discriminatory approach makes the coverage available to all employees regardless of their health. Employees are free to accept or decline the benefit. The opportunity to apply for insurance is open to all, and each employee makes the decision individually. The decision is not based upon health status but instead upon the employee's true need. This non-underwriting concept protects the employer and the offer from discrimination.

Although a guaranteed-issue offer is advantageous, it is important to take care of the carrier, the employer and all involved by insisting on mandatory meetings with the employees. It's important to see everyone and have them either sign up or sign off on a waiver form. Some employers may initially balk at this idea, but when they understand the carrier's view of adverse selection and that this process protects them as an employer against future repercussions, they usually understand and acquiesce. An employer certainly does not want an employee's spouse to come back after the employee has passed away and say, "If we knew that this coverage was offered, we would have bought it." A simple yet mandatory sign-up sheet, with that particular employee's sign-off signature, eliminates that conversation.

Even if the employees come in and say, "No thanks, not interested," at least we have an opportunity to see them and perhaps change their mind or educate them about the offer. As they're signing the waiver form, we initiate some sort of conversation. By quickly reading and adapting to their personality styles, we usually turn them around. They may not have been interested in life insurance initially, but once they sit down, they might see the value in a child rider, spouse coverage or perhaps another product that is being offered.

Value-added riders can be presented along with the base life plan to create customized policies that address many concerns besides death. For example, a long-term care rider, when attached to a life policy, allows the insured to access their death benefit to cover expenses associated with nursing home care, assisted living care, home health care or adult day care. Some carriers feature an extension benefit that allows access to the death benefit not only once, but twice. With the long-term care rider, employees enjoy two highly utilized coverages for the price of one. Long-term care has more sizzle than life insurance because the insured can potentially use the benefit instead of the survivors. However, many people cannot qualify for or afford a true stand-alone plan. But if the voluntary life plan, along with the long-term care rider, is a guaranteed-issue offer, what was once elusive and expensive becomes affordable and accessible. Riders are an excellent way to arouse interest in an otherwise disinterested employee.

What Harry Left Sally

Many years ago, we conducted an enrollment at a large car dealership. The one-on-one meetings were mandatory and we saw close to 98 percent of the employees. On the last day, there were still a few stragglers, who were either totally oblivious to the enrollment event or who were deliberately hiding. We were tired and anxious to wrap up, but made it a point to track down Harry, the service guy, who was tucked way back in a broken-down garage behind the main building. Harry was greasy and gruff and said, “I have no need for life insurance. I’m happily single and I’m busy right now.” He signed the waiver form but his interest piqued as I casually mentioned the long-term care idea. “So, since you’re single, who would look after you if something happened and you needed assistance on a daily basis?” I asked as he handed back the pen. Less than 15 minutes later, Harry bought a $10-weekly premium and tossed the waiver form.

Two years later, a call came into the office from a woman who said, “This is Sally Smith. My ex-husband passed away two months ago and I am at his house cleaning out his belongings. He keeps getting a bill from XYZ insurance company. What is this all about?” Her call prompted us to contact the man’s employer, the large car dealership, and sure enough, Harry had passed away. No one had yet notified our office or the insurance carrier. We checked our files for Harry’s information and found that he had life insurance coverage and that the beneficiary was Sally Smith, his ex-wife.

We returned Sally's call to tell her the news. She wept as she spoke, "Even though we were no longer married, Harry promised that by August, he would find me a warm place to live this winter. I live in an old house with little heat and no insulation. It's so cold and drafty here in the winter. And now that he's gone he still is able to keep his promise to me through this policy money."

Imagine if we had not ventured into that greasy garage to track down the remaining two percent of the disinterested employees? A passion for people and their outcomes is what the business of worksite marketing is all about. Every life matters.

The Harry story has additional value as it pertains to the agent or broker side of selling universal life, and to the need to run an organized and professional operation. Harry was two months behind on his premium payments not only because he passed away, but also because the dealership was always months behind in remitting premium. When the dealership finally paid the premiums directly to the carrier, there was a good chance that the entire premium per person would be applied as one month's payment instead of two.

All too often, employers remit payments with little or no corroborating paperwork, making it difficult, if not impossible, to allocate premiums correctly. For example, Harry had a monthly deduction of $40. The dealership remitted $80 to the carrier for July and August. But the carrier applied the entire $80 to July. If this were to go on for several months, the universal life policy would become over-funded beyond its target premium. But most agents have no idea about any of this because they do not see the bills, the checks or the paperwork and have little time to decipher commission statements.

So what does this mean to an agent or broker? Based on how the contract reads with the carrier, it can have two very serious financial consequences:

1. Once premiums exceed the allowed cumulative target premiums, first-year commissions may not be paid on the excess. So if premiums are misapplied for whatever reason, agents may lose out on rightfully earned commissions.
2. Premiums received after the 13th or 14th month of the first deductions may not qualify for first-year commissions. Once again, if the employer is late in remitting premiums or if posting is delayed for any reason, agents may lose out on commissions.

Therefore, it behooves agents and brokers to read and understand every word in their contract. See to it that the carrier posts premiums in a timely manner, keep up with clients and their payment habits and, better yet, set up an internal system to track billing, payments and commissions. Try to separate multiple months with individual checks and reconciliation paperwork to make it clear how the money should be applied. Then track the transaction with commission statements, if at all possible. It is important not only for commission purposes, but for the client as well, that life insurance premiums are posted accurately and in a timely fashion.

A Case for Universal Life

Harry had been gone for two months before our office knew about it. The dealership was consistently late with their premium payments. Had Harry's policy been a term or whole-life policy, the chance of it remaining in force by the time Sally called is small.

Last year we received a similar call from the head of human resources at a construction company we have enrolled for more than 10 years. This time the insured, John, passed away only days before the call. The HR director wanted to know if John had any policies with us. He saw that there were deductions, but didn't know if any were for a life policy. Upon retrieving John's file we saw that he had a cancer plan and disability coverage with us. Also in the file was a release form that he had signed two years prior, authorizing the cancellation of his life insurance premiums with a note that said, "Can't afford."

John had paid premiums into his universal life policy for three years before he decided to cancel. Knowing how universal life policies work, we called the carrier to see if by chance the policy was still in force. Even after two years without premium payments, this policy was still alive. We immediately called the HR director who excitedly called John's wife. She had been prepared to sell her wedding ring to pay for the funeral. Now all she had to do was fill out a claim form.

Imagine once again what would have happened if we had not done our job correctly? Because each client has a file, we had a release form that indicated John's cancellation of his life policy. Looking back at billing sheets, we saw that he had paid premiums for three years prior to cancellation. Armed with this information, we knew to call the carrier to inquire about the status of the policy. I wonder how many claims never get paid because the agent or broker didn't know, didn't have the time or didn't care to have processes in place to ensure that each client is treated like he or she matters.

The Digger

Because of the multitude of experiences I've had that exemplify the need to see each and every employee, I personally attend each enrollment. My staff calls me "the digger." When employees dodge and hide from the enrollment process or the enrollers themselves, I seek them out, make friends, find their need and explain why it is most likely in their best interest to spend a few moments with the benefits counselors. While it's easy to sit and wait for the majority of employees to show up for their meetings and leave an enrollment citing your "best effort," experience has shown that those unseen employees just might be the ones who need our help the most.

So when agents seek my counsel and ask about my move from the board-room to the break room, I tell them, "To do the right job in worksite, you have to do all of it. It's not only necessary to understand the types of life insurance and other products. Care for your clients as people. Take the time, effort and financial resources to build a business. Understand how every aspect of your business works. Do all of the dirty work. Dig the employees out of their corners, create in-house systems to copy applications and service requests, take phone calls, and track billing and premiums. People's lives and futures are at stake. Selling life insurance matters because it impacts generations of families you will never meet. And that is why it doesn't stop with the sale. You've taken the time to offer an important piece of financial security to thousands of people. See it through to the end. You and your business are important. You matter. Your clients matter. Life matters."

Bob Noe began his career in the insurance and financial services industry with a major life insurance carrier in 1968. He sold life insurance and securities and consistently received the company's highest awards and distinctions. As CEO of Noe and Associates, Bob and his staff specialized in the individual large-case market. He was elected president of the Morristown, Tennessee, Life Underwriters Association for four terms (1974, 1976, 1983, 1989) and has received NAIFA's National Sales Achievement Award and NAIFA's National Quality Award on numerous occasions.

In 1995, Bob co-founded Millennium Benefits Group Insurance Agency, Inc. and MBG Enrollment Consulting Services with the desire to offer more life insurance to a wider, underinsured worksite audience. In this capacity, he has been a leading producer for several major life insurance carriers. Bob is also a Qualifying and Life Member of the Million Dollar Round Table, having been named to the Honor Roll and the Court of the Table.

Robert H. Noe
CEO
Millennium Benefits Group
46 Chagrin Plaza #103
Chagrin Falls, OH 44022
Phone: 440-286-2010
Fax: 440-286-2084
Email: mbg@mbenefitsgroup.com
Website: www.mbenefitsgroup.com

Chapter Seven

Disability Insurance: Marketing the Benefits of Cost Control and Absence Management

NEICIEE DURRENCE
Vice President, Voluntary Practice & Product Management
Unum

To understand why worksite disability benefits have a vital place in today's employee benefits marketplace, it's important to look at the economic trends and demographic changes that are having a significant impact on employers.

The benefits budget squeeze

It's often said that the three key factors to real estate success are "location, location, location." In today's benefits sphere, the key factors can easily be summed up as "cost control, cost control, cost control." Employers must rein in benefits expenses while maintaining a benefits package that will effectively recruit and retain top performers.

It's no secret that rising health care costs continue to eat up the majority of the benefits pie, often eclipsing available funds for other necessary benefits. But the secret to success in worksite disability benefits is understanding that the newest, most innovative products and plan designs can actually *help* employers as they struggle with costs.

The employer's point of view

When you consider the facts, it's easy to see why today's employers cannot ignore the impact of workplace disability:

- Almost three in 10 workers entering the workforce today will become disabled before retirement.[1]

- In 2006, unscheduled absences cost some large employers an estimated $850,000 in direct payroll.[2]
- Disabling injuries and illnesses account for 55 percent of employee absences.[3]

That's an expensive problem. Providing a creative solution is priceless. To present it successfully to customers, you need a firm grasp on the pain points they are facing in addition to the health care crisis.

Underlying trends

A number of eye-opening trends have put the issue of disability on the front burner for many employers. Consider these facts:

- **Workplace disabilities are on the rise.** Since 2000, the number of disabled workers in America has increased by 35 percent, a trend that is expected to continue.[4] This has a tremendous impact not just on absenteeism, but on workplace productivity as well. In fact, Unum claims data shows that any increase in incidence can significantly impact claim costs, particularly for larger employers.

- **The workforce is growing older.** The average workforce age in 2012 is projected to be 41.4 years, an increase from 40 in 2002 and 36.6 in 1992.[5] And the incidence of chronic health conditions increases dramatically with age.[6] In fact, according to the Employee Benefits Research Institute, age 60 is the new 50 in today's workplace.[7] Disability benefits that offer return-to-work assistance can identify workplace adaptations that can help older workers return to a productive lifestyle. They offer a distinct advantage to employers with a steadily graying workforce.

- **Obesity in the United States is an epidemic.** A national study conducted at Duke University revealed that obese employees have 13 times more lost workdays due to work-related injuries than their healthy counterparts, with average medical costs around $50,000, compared to about $7,000 for non-obese workers.[8] This trend has made it important for employers to offer disability benefits paired with a disease-management program.

- **Many of the leading causes of disability are related to obesity or aging.** An analysis of claims data shows that aside from normal pregnancy, the leading causes of long- and short-term disability are often directly related to obesity, such as cancer and cardiovascular diseases, or are more likely to occur with aging, such as joint, muscle or connective-tissue diseases and back injuries.

The top five causes of long-term disability:

1. Cancer
2. Complications of pregnancy
3. Joint/muscle/connective-tissue diseases
4. Back injuries
5. Cardiovascular diseases

The top five causes of short-term disability:

1. Normal pregnancy
2. Injuries (not including back injuries)
3. Digestive/intestinal diseases
4. Reproductive/urinary system diseases
5. Pregnancy complications

Unum claims data shows that the median claimant age is increasing by five months per year and there is a sharp increase in claims incidence for ages 50+.

- **Family demographics are changing.** In generations past, an employee suffering from a disabling illness or injury could rely on a spouse or grown children to help provide care and manage the financial impact. In today's workplace, however, married couples are the minority,[10] and fewer people are choosing to have children.[11] The personal savings rate now hovers at or below zero and many employees can not afford to live for even a month without an income stream during a period of disability.[12] Today's comprehensive range of disability products allows employees to choose and pay for only the coverage that fits their unique needs.

- **The talent pool is shrinking fast.** Approximately 60 percent of human resource executives surveyed said they see signs of a talent shortage, while nearly 10 percent said they expect to see a shortage before the end of the decade.[13] The competition for top performers is fierce. To stay in the game, employers need to offer what workers want. And research shows that employee benefits

– along with pay – remain at the top of the list of factors that determine U.S. employees' job satisfaction. In fact, 65 percent of employees surveyed cite benefits as "a very important aspect of job satisfaction."[14]

Taken together, these factors can create financial strain for any company that attempts to shoulder the full disability risk for its employees. They show the need for:

- Cost stabilization. By integrating employer-paid group disability benefits with voluntary coverage, employers can stabilize costs, even if faced with a period of adverse selection experience. And they can offer a richer benefits package without negatively impacting the bottom line.
- Level premiums. Cost is also a growing concern for employees, as they grapple with everything from skyrocketing medical co-payments to rising gasoline prices. Voluntary coverage offers workers financial protection with level premiums that, unlike the price at the pump, won't constantly increase.

How trends reconfigure the industry

These demographic, economic and workplace trends have enormous implications for emerging disability plan designs as carriers search for new innovations that will position them ahead of a groundswell of changes. As a result, we see these trends emerging among the thought leaders in disability coverage:

- Products that are more flexible in design and more employee-need focused
- Growth in voluntary plan designs as opposed to traditional employer-paid group coverage
- Offerings that include employer-paid, 100-percent employee-paid and shared-funding options
- Employees given the responsibility for choosing the coverage they need and helping to manage the costs
- Cutting-edge innovation in technology, including self-service online enrollments and streamlined administration, as demanded by employers
- Complete absence and productivity management programs included with disability coverage, especially requested by large employers

- A new world of attractive, educational employee benefits communications on disability products that use clear language to explain options without insurance buzzwords

The shift from 100-percent employer-funded benefits to shared funding and 100-percent employee-paid benefits has been well received in the marketplace thanks to the convergence of:

- The continuing cost-shifting trend
- The health care consumerism movement
- Political propositions of an "ownership society"

To some extent, the growth of cost-sharing varies within certain market segments. We have seen more 100-percent employee-paid plans within specific industries such as education, health care and legal.

Giving customers a competitive edge

What drives an employer's chief interest in a disability plan design and funding options? In most cases, the employer wants to know the most elusive of facts: What is my competition offering?

In order to keep valuable employees from being "poached" by rival companies or to recruit the best talent in the industry, an employer needs a good grasp on the kinds of benefits top candidates may be offered by the competition.

Brokers are often viewed as an important source for this benchmark data. The key is to work with a carrier that can offer a significant database of sales and claims data. This information can help employers make the final decision about what they need to offer in order to be truly competitive in the marketplace.

The face of today's disability plan

So what does an innovative, comprehensive disability plan look like?

1. It starts with basic coverage for long-term and short-term disability.
    - For example, a basic group plan may cover 60 percent of an employee's salary during a period of disability.

- An employee-paid voluntary plan offers coverage based on a flat dollar amount, sold in small increments (such as $100), that offers coverage up to a set benefit amount (such as $50,000) with a cap that equals a set percentage of the employee's salary.
- Vital to plan design: Short-term and long-term disability plans must dovetail completely to avoid gaps, or an overlap, in coverage.

2. Employees have the option to "buy up" more coverage to meet their needs. This may provide additional coverage, such as 75 percent of the employee's salary, and a higher maximum benefit amount than basic coverage.
   - A significant advantage of base buy-up plans: Voluntary benefits with a base of employer funding or those that are selected and endorsed by the employer generate higher participation and higher persistency rates.[15]
   - The employee advantage to these plans: Workers have the flexibility to choose how much coverage they need and can afford.
3. Executives and highly compensated individuals can choose completely voluntary individual disability coverage. This is typically of interest to those who earn at least $75,000 a year.
   - This coverage provides additional coverage beyond salary replacement, covering other income such as bonuses and commissions.
4. Voluntary employee-paid products, such as accident and critical illness, can help round out a comprehensive disability plan and provide the additional protection employees need. These plans can play an essential role in protecting employees from the financial devastation that can result from a disabling illness or injury.

If we build it, will they come?

It's clear that employees are going to be asked to assume more responsibility for choosing and funding the insurance protection they need. Will they be willing to do so? Surveys show they are ready to step up to the plate:

- Employees say disability insurance is a necessity.
  — A Harris Interactive survey found that an overwhelming majority of workers polled – 97 percent – say they believe they need some level of income replacement in the event of a disability.[16]

Employees understand the financial repercussions of a disability. Fifty-six percent of U.S. adults surveyed say they would not be able to pay their bills or meet expenses if they became disabled and could not work for one year or longer.[17]

- Employees are prepared to share the bill for coverage offered at the workplace.
  — Disability insurance is the most popular voluntary "employee-paid" benefit offered by employers.[18]

Like their employers, employees seem ready to welcome a cost-effective solution they can afford.

The art of integrating group and voluntary disability plans

While it is vital for employers to offer employees an array of disability benefits, it's helpful if the same carrier provides them all. If not, it can be difficult to properly integrate the plans and align the coverage.

A truly effective disability plan offers tools that simplify employee-absence management, including the tracking of FMLA leave time and its interaction with disability leave. Consider this case study:

Industry: Computer manufacturing

Challenge: *A fast-growing company was experiencing a high level of absenteeism and wanted to lower lost-time costs while improving productivity.*

Solution: *An integrated disability program with absence-management services combining:*

- Long-term disability insurance
- Short-term disability insurance
- Alignment with workers' compensation claims
- Family and Medical Leave Act tracking
- Comparative reporting and analysis tools for all leaves

Results: *The first year of the new plan yielded the following benefits:*

- 32-percent reduction in lost time
- 20-percent reduction in workers' compensation claims duration
- Median disability claims duration of 19 days, which is significantly lower than the industry median of 43 days
- 36-percent reduction in the length of integrated leaves

Bottom line: $4.6 million in cost savings associated with the reduction in leave time for the first year of the integrated disability program.

Here are some other examples of how significant an integrated disability program can be.

The danger of de-motivation

Consider the case of an employee on disability whose short-term and long-term disability plans overlap because of a lack of integration. For a period of time, the employee would actually collect 110 percent of his usual salary. The result is zero incentive to return to the workplace, as the employee actually receives a "raise" while not working at all. To avoid this scenario, it's important that the elimination period for long-term disability coverage dovetails with the length of the benefit period for short-term disability coverage.

Lapses in coverage

On the other hand, consider the dilemma of an employee battling cancer whose short-term disability coverage ends after six weeks. However, the employee must wait another six weeks before her long-term disability coverage begins.

During the interim, the employee, who is receiving no income, is likely faced with thousands of dollars in medical co-payments, coinsurance and other costs. To avoid such a gap in coverage, the short-term disability plan must dovetail with the long-term plan. If it doesn't, that lack of integration creates a situation that is *opposite* the intent of disability insurance, which is designed to ensure that employees on claim receive a portion of their earnings during a crisis time when their expenses are likely to increase.

With a gap in income, an employee might not have the financial resources to receive treatment or might be forced to take on medical debt that is difficult to ever pay off. In fact, a national study of low- and middle-income households that took on medical debt revealed that their credit card debt is 46 percent higher than that of their peers, with an average debt of $11,623.[19] This adds an extra element of anxiety when employees are already dealing with the stress of a disabling illness or injury.

While the second scenario illustrates how critical disability benefits are to an employee's overall benefits program, it also highlights the potential for additional voluntary benefits. By offering products such as critical illness, accident or cancer insurance, employers can give employees the opportunity to further protect their finances from serious health events, at little or no cost to the company.

Customized coverage for a changing workforce

Today's employee insurance needs are as diverse as the changing face of the workforce itself. Integrated disability coverage allows an employer to tailor its disability coverage to meet the needs of all employees, at any income level or stage of life.

- For example, consider a school district with a high percentage of female workers of child-bearing age. By offering a voluntary short-term disability program, an employer can offer an employee who is planning a family the opportunity to purchase the coverage she needs to spend time with her newborn baby.
- Or, consider a mid-sized hospital with a large number of highly compensated medical professionals. Offering a buy-up to basic disability coverage can help protect a larger portion of income for those who need it. Adding a voluntary individual plan with a definition of disability that is defined by medical specialty provides important coverage above and beyond "own-occupation" coverage.

Data-driven answers

Today's variations in product plan design and funding options are born of in-depth research and analysis, from extensive sales data to focus groups. The resulting approach gives employers and employees the innovative solutions they need to meet some of today's toughest challenges.

For employers they offer:

- Help controlling benefits costs
- A richer benefits package to recruit better job candidates and retain valuable employees

- Help maintaining a healthier workforce, which can help lower health care costs.

For employees, they provide protection from the financial fallout of a disabling illness or injury with flexible plans to fit any budget.

This new approach to disability benefits does more than just meet the demands of the top trends affecting businesses today. It has been developed with the foresight to plan for the emerging benefits challenges of tomorrow's workplace.

Sources:

1 Social Security Administration, Fact Sheet, January 31, 2007.

2 CCH and Harris Interactive, "2006 CCH Unscheduled Absence Survey," October 2006.

3 Employee Benefit News-JHA 2005 Absence Management Survey, results reported in Benefit-News.com, "Big-picture benefits: Integrating FMLA and disability claims data helps reduce absenteeism," by Chris Silva, September 2006.

4 Council for Disability Awareness, "Misinformation, Poor Planning Can Threaten Financial Security," March 7, 2007.

5 Bureau of Labor Statistics, Feb. 2004 Monthly Labor Review, Table 7. Based on the Current Population Survey, U.S. Census. The most recent year for which statistics are currently available.

6 The Commonwealth Fund, "Health Coverage for Aging Baby Boomers: Findings from The Commonwealth Fund Survey Of Older Adults." By Sara R. Collins, Karen, Davis, Cathy Schoen, Michelle M. Doty, and Jennifer L. Kriss, January 2006.

7 Employee Benefits Research Institute (EBRI), "Employment Status of Workers Age 55 or Older," By Craig Copeland, August 2007, Vol. 28, No. 8, page 2.

8 Archives of Internal Medicine, "Obesity and Workers' Compensation Results From the Duke Health and Safety Surveillance System," sponsored by the National Institute for Occupational Safety and Health, April 2007.

10 The New York Times, "To Be Married Means to Be Outnumbered," October 15, 2006.

11 The Washington Post, "Childless: Some by Chance, Some by Choice," by Nancy Rome, Nov 27, 2006.

12 U.S. Department of Commerce, Bureau of Economic Analysis, August 2007.

13 Society for Human Resource Management, "Some Companies Face Talent Dearth; Verdict Still Out for Others," August 2006.

14 SHRM, Workplace Trends Program, "Workplace Vision: Benefit Trends and Employee Satisfaction," Issue 3, 2007.

15 LIMRA, 2007.

16 Harris Interactive study commissioned by Unum, August 2006. National Association of Insurance Commissioners, "Majority of Americans Unprepared for Financial Impact of Disability," February 28, 2007.

17 National Association of Insurance Commissioners, "Majority of Americans Unprepared for Financial Impact of Disability," February 28, 2007.

18 AON Consulting, "What's Hot and What's Not in Voluntary Benefits," January 2006.

19 Demos/The Access Project, "Borrowing to Stay Healthy: How Credit Card Debt Is Related to Medical Expenses," January 2007.

Neiciee Durrence is vice president of voluntary practice and product management for Unum in Chattanooga, Tennessee. In this capacity, she is responsible for coordination of the cross-functional management team focused on voluntary benefits growth and profit objectives, as well as product development activities supporting the group life and voluntary benefits portfolios.

Neiciee joined the former Provident organization in 1984 and has served in a variety of roles in sales, customer service, marketing and product development. In 1999, Provident and Unum merged, and now conduct business under the Unum brand. Over the course of Neiciee's career, the company has enjoyed significant growth in the worksite market, emerging as a leader in voluntary employee benefits. Unum is recognized for its strength in benefit communication and enrollment technology via plane.biz (which was initially developed under Neiciee's leadership), as well as the streamlined customer acquisition and ongoing administrative support employers and employees demand.

Neiciee is an active member of various industry organizations including the Mass Marketing Institute (current board member), NACII (former board member), Workplace Benefits Association, VEEB (former board member), and the LIMRA Worksite Advisory Committee. She frequently participates as a guest speaker at industry events and has published articles in select trade publications including *Broker World*, *National Underwriter* and *Advisor Today.*

Neiciee Durrence
Vice President, Voluntary Practice & Product Management
Unum
1 Fountain Square
Chattanooga, TN 37402
Phone: 423-294-7204
Fax: 423-294-1301
Email: ndurrence@unum.com
Website: www.unum.com

CHAPTER EIGHT

Critical Illness Insurance: Coverage That Can Save Your Life

ROBERT S. SHESTACK, CES
NATIONAL PRACTICE LEADER: VOLUNTARY BENEFITS
TRION

The employee benefits arena has undergone a dramatic change in just a few short years. Employers continue to offer core benefit programs such as affordably priced life and disability protection, but rising health care costs make it difficult to offer comprehensive health insurance coverage. For some employers, rising health care costs means increasing employees' contributions to their health insurance program. Accordingly, the benefits offered within existing medical plans, such as deductibles and co-payments, are increasing. Employees are then faced with additional out-of-pocket expenses.

Offsetting these rising insurance costs is not an employer's only concern. It is also becoming more difficult to attract and retain top workforce talent when balancing the cost of providing a solid employee benefit program. To combat these issues, many employers are beginning to offer additional employer-paid coverage, such as critical illness and cancer programs, to supplement their core life and disability offerings.

According to a 2004 National Association for Critical Illness Insurance (NACII) study made public in the *National Underwriter*, approximately 411,000 pure lump-sum critical illness policies were in force. That number continues to increase. Critical illness has the potential to surpass disability insurance as the second leading voluntary benefits program purchased at the worksite, while life insurance remains a solid number one. Clearly, critical illness programs are fast becoming a new cornerstone in employer-paid programs.

Thanks to the many advancements made in medical technology over the past 100 years, people are living longer—as much as 30 years longer than a century ago—and today have an average lifespan of 77 years. And with current medical technologies, surgical methodologies and prescription medications, Americans' lifespans will continue to increase, furthering the need for employers to offer critical illness insurance.

What is critical illness insurance?

Critical illness insurance was first created by Dr. Marius Barnard, a member of the team that performed the world's first human-to-human heart transplant in South Africa. Dr. Barnard was inspired to create the first critical illness insurance program by the financial hardship he saw his patients endure after treating their critical illnesses. He convinced the South African insurance companies to introduce a new type of insurance to cover critical illnesses, arguing that, as a medical doctor, "he can repair a man physically, but only insurers can repair a patient's finances." As a result of Dr. Barnard's efforts, on October 6, 1983, the first critical illness insurance policy was launched. And, although less than 100 policies were initially sold (mostly in the UK), according to the NACII, the number of critical illness polices sold in the United States in 2005 was approximately 170,000.

How does critical illness insurance work?

Critical illness insurance is designed to pay a lump-sum benefit directly to the insured—not to hospitals or doctors—upon the diagnosis of a covered critical illness. Funds from the policy can help the recipient direct his or her own treatment of specified diseases and cover unanticipated out-of-pocket expenses. Typical critical illnesses covered under this type of policy, depending on the insurance carrier are (including but not limited to):

- Heart attack
- End-stage renal (kidney) failure
- Paralysis
- Burns
- Coma
- Stroke

- Alzheimer's
- Coronary artery bypass surgery
- Major organ transplant
- Cancer

The critical illness insurance benefits paid are generally used to help fill gaps in major medical insurance, although many who purchase critical illness coverage do so to protect their financial assets. Critical illness insurance can also pay for caregivers, special medical equipment and transportation expenses, as well as an annual health screening benefit to help in early detection and treatment of the aforementioned illnesses.

Doesn't core health insurance cover critical illness?

In August 2007, the U.S. Housing and Household Economic Statistics Division indicated that 250 million Americans (84 percent) had health insurance, while 47 million (16 percent) did not. For the 250 million participating in a medical plan, having major medical coverage for a critical condition may not be enough, as the residual effects of surviving a critical illness are almost endless. Many insured Americans experience serious financial problems even when major medical coverage exists.

According to the American Cancer Society, one in two men and one in three women will be diagnosed with cancer in their lifetimes, with an average survival rate of 62 percent for all types of cancer. The increase in survivor rates over the years is the good news. The bad news often comes in the midst of, or just following, a successful battle with cancer. Survivors and their families can be financially shattered by non-hospital and other expenses not covered by health insurance. An incorrect public assumption is that good health insurance will afford adequate financial protection in the event of a medical crisis. That is a dangerous assumption to make in a serious medical crisis, because the loss of income and increased non-medical expenses can be devastating.

According to a recent study by *The Journal of Health Affairs*, more than 2 million Americans who filed for bankruptcy in 2004 (representing half of all U.S. bankruptcies), did so in part due to overwhelming medical bills or other financial consequences of illness or injury. And 76 percent of those families studied had major medical insurance, but were "underinsured" to cover all critical illness costs. The average out-of-pocket costs for the illnesses that led to bankruptcy were $13,460. For those with cancer, that number was more than $35,800.

Clearly, we need to be concerned about the residual financial risks that exist even when we have health insurance. The reality is that health insurance may only cover care and treatment of a critical illness. The complementary and supplementary solution to health insurance is a critical illness insurance policy.

Critical illness insurance pays for crisis-related bills not covered by major medical insurance, including:

- Medical insurance deductibles
- Prescription drug co-payments
- Rehabilitation
- Alternative treatments
- Extra childcare costs
- Transportation to health facilities
- Private nursing home or home health care
- Preventive health screenings
- Family travel for visits
- Replacement of lost income when your illness forces you to miss work
- Mortgages and other loans
- Daily living expenses

But if my family and I are healthy, why do I need critical illness insurance?

Marie Killian, J.D., whose chapter on wellness can be read in this book, specifically addresses the importance of wellness programs, which drastically reduce the likelihood of a critical illness. But until wellness programs become a part of our everyday lives, 5.7 out of every 10 Americans will die from illnesses such as heart disease, cancer and stroke. If diabetes, the leading cause of kidney disease, is included, that number increases to six out of every 10 people or 60 percent, according to the U.S. National Center on Health Statistics*.

When critical illness touched my life

Critical illness affected my family when my 34-year-old wife was diagnosed with stage II breast cancer. I was 33 years old with two beautiful young children. Previously, I had naively believed that my family had nothing to worry about when it came to a serious medical condition. I was certain that if a critical illness affected us, we were safe from financial risk because I had excellent health insurance coverage. Armed with my actuarial degree from Temple University and 11 years of practical experience (at that time), I calculated that the odds were in my favor for my family to remain financially secure in the wake of my wife's cancer treatment. How wrong I was.

More than a decade of crunching numbers and telling others how important insurance was did not prepare me for what happened to my family. Of course we were scared and my primary concern was for my wife's life. Although the financial aspect of the disease did concern me, I was comforted by the fact that I had a comprehensive medical plan. After all, my insurance plan covered eight months of treatment, chemotherapy, radiation therapy, prescription medications, hospital stays and surgeries. But it was the costs that occurred after her discharge and treatments that nearly devastated my family.

I had to rent a medical bed, which was not covered by insurance, and I had to pay for people to help take care of the kids. I had to get my wife to her daily therapy treatments while also getting my daughter to the bus stop in time, arranging for someone to care for my four-year-old son, cleaning the house, doing the laundry and preparing our meals (while running a benefits administration business). I had no idea how much work my wife did.

Even after all of the medical bills, which were nearly completely covered, we still accrued more than $10,000 in expenses. But most importantly, my wife is going into her ninth cancer-free year. But my story doesn't end there. In February 2007, only one day after my 42nd birthday, doctors diagnosed my then 12-year-old son, Kyle, with type-I diabetes, which is a leading cause of kidney failure in the United States. Thanks to the critical illness insurance I purchased for my family a few years earlier, my son and our entire family have some added protection. Kyle is basically uninsurable. He continues to adapt as well as can be expected for a young boy and manages his diabetes like an Olympic champion. My daughter, Brianna, is healthy and we continue to actively support the Susan G. Komen Breast Cancer Foundation as well as the Juvenile Diabetes Research Foundation.

My story is just one of thousands out there. Remember the statistic that medical bills cause 50 percent of the bankruptcies in this country and 77 percent of those who filed had major medical insurance? It is about the expenses that arise after the medical bills are paid.

Why buy critical illness insurance?

Modern medicine has dramatically increased our chances of surviving a serious illness. According to a 2002 report by the American Heart Association, 88 percent of heart-attack patients younger than 65 are able to return to work, with some limitations, and more than 6 million stroke victims are alive today.

A quality supplemental benefits program can make all the difference in the world when it comes to the financial survival of a working family in the midst of a medical crisis. The cash generated by such a plan is always in addition to existing health, life or disability coverage, and can be spent in any way. Benefits are paid directly to the policy owner, who can choose how and where to spend the money without constraints, conditions or limitations.

The average American might tell you that he or she does not smoke, exercises daily, eats low-cholesterol foods, and has perfect blood pressure and excellent blood-sugar levels. But we are kidding ourselves if we think the average American is *that* healthy. Exercising regularly, eating healthfully and not using tobacco are commendable achievements, but they aren't always enough to overcome genetic predispositions and other critical illness risks.

How much does critical illness insurance cost and is it worth it?

I argue passionately about the need for supplemental insurance programs such as critical illness. I know from experience that expenses don't end with the last hospital bill. Unfortunately, I did not have critical illness insurance for my wife, but if I did, it would have covered all of the expenses that we incurred. Today, I have $65,000 of critical illness insurance on myself, $60,000 on my wife, and $10,000 for each child. The annual cost of these family policies is around $900 ($450 for my policy) and it would take more than 144 years for my premium payments to equal the lump sum benefits I would receive. In fact, statistics suggest that I have close to an 80 percent chance of having a critical illness in my lifetime. So if I do live to the average age of 77, the premiums I will have paid will represent only 24 percent of the benefit I will most likely receive.

Statistics show that six out of 10 (seven out of 10 if you include diabetes) of your friends and family members will suffer from a critical illness in their lifetime, which could be financially devastating. Fortunately, my wife's illness did not bankrupt us, but many others are not so fortunate. So learn from our personal tragedy. If your employer offers critical illness insurance, buy it. If you are an employer, offer it. And if you are a benefits consultant, recommend it.

---

*National Center for Health Statistics: Deaths/Mortality, October 4, 2007 (http://www.cdc.gov/nchs/fastats/deaths.htm)

Rob Shestack, CES, is the voluntary benefits national practice leader for Trion, one of the nation's largest privately held employee benefits firms. Prior to joining Trion, Rob was senior vice president of strategic development for Univers Workplace Benefits where he developed several proprietary voluntary benefits as well as created innovative benefit enrollment strategies.

A 20-year veteran of the industry, Rob has a bachelor's degree in actuarial science and is a resident expert on Section 125 and ERISA compliance. He currently serves on the executive committee and advisory board for the Workplace Benefits Association and has been nominated as president-elect and will lead the association in 2010. Rob and the businesses he has managed have won numerous awards, including two Philadelphia Business Journal Awards and a Wharton Business School Award. In June 2007, Rob was featured on the cover of *Benefits Selling Magazine* and has been published numerous times on various topics such as voluntary benefits and ERISA compliance. Organizations such as the United Way have recognized him for his charitable and community service. Rob and his wife, Debbie, have two children, Brianna and Kyle. They reside in Southern New Jersey near Philadelphia.

Robert S. Shestack, CES
National Practice Leader: Voluntary Benefits
Trion
2300 Renaissance Boulevard
King of Prussia, PA 19406
Phone: 856-437-8555
Mobile: 856-278-5454
Fax: 856-437-8555
Email: rshestack@trion.com
Website: www.trion.com

Chapter Nine

Demographics Say It's Time For LTCI

CARROLL S. GOLDEN
CLU, CHFC, CMFC, CLTC, LTCP, CASL, ALMI, ACS
Vice President Sales & Marketing
Transamerica Life Insurance Company
Long Term Care Division

In order to take its place at the voluntary worksite table, long-term care insurance (LTCI) will have to show up appropriately dressed for the occasion. Many voluntary products, such as life insurance, are easy to explain, as they only require one trigger and the need is inevitable and universal. The challenge for LTCI is not just establishing a need, but recognizing that there are multiple needs that take many forms. So, while LTCI is still new to the voluntary employee benefits world, carriers and distribution outlets have already had to change the product's presentation in response to the challenges presented by the market.

Everyone wants a simple, easy-to-understand product, but that desire has not necessarily led to successful LTCI distribution. Carriers, distributors and the government have come to realize that what is needed is a product suitable for various distribution formats as well as various prospects. To meet this challenge, the LTCI industry has been responsible for seeking and creating additional solutions to satisfy the need for long-term care options.

The good news is that things have come a long way since the 1980s when LTCI coverage was first introduced to the market. Early LTCI policies were based upon benefit triggers similar to those of Medicaid. They were focused on nursing-home (facility) coverage and sold to "older" people.

Almost all policies sold in today's marketplace are tax-qualified LTCI (TQ-LTCI) products affording a wide range of individualization. There are usually two types of benefit triggers: 1. An inability to perform two out of six “activities of daily living” (transferring, toileting, continence, bathing, eating and dressing), and 2. A severe cognitive impairment that warrants care for the safety and well-being of the individual. The policy-holder does not have to meet both triggers but rather one or the other.

There are several differences in the methods used to access funds. Basically, all are variations of the following four models and all are limited by the benefit package that the insured purchased which could include exhaustion of funds:

Reimbursement: Policyholders lay out the expenses and the LTCI company reimburses the policyholders.

Indemnity: Policyholders receive the full daily benefit, regardless of incurred expenses, for as long as they qualify.

Hybrid: A combination of reimbursement and indemnity.

Cash: No receipts are required and policyholders spend the money as they see fit. In order to qualify for tax advantages, careful record-keeping may be necessary.

At first, all LTCI policies were “stand-alone” policies that addressed only the financial implications of LTCI coverage. Soon, carriers began to recognize that in order for the coverage to appeal to a wider and younger audience, they would have to offer more expanded coverage, and so “combination” policies were introduced.

Today the worksite market supports both stand-alone and combination products:

1. Stand-Alone Products
   a. MultiLife (ILTCI)
   b. True Group (GLTCI)
2. Combination Products

Let’s take a look at the differences.

MultiLife (ILTCI)

MultiLife is basically a grouping of individual LTCI policies. Under-writing rules, commissions and application formats vary by size and by type of group, expected participation, HR and carrier administration, operational capabilities, and enrollment criteria.

True Group (GLTCI)

True Group enrollments are usually similar in format to the installation of other voluntary group benefits, bypass the majority of state-distinct regulations and are guaranteed issue (GI).

GLTCI GI offers coverage to all employees, regardless of their health. GLTCI is priced with a load for low voluntary participation, underwriting concessions (healthy people may subsidize less healthy people, which may boost the cost for everyone) and possible adverse selection issues. A few group policies offer spousal discounts and fewer offer special benefits, such as shared-care coverage, which allows spouses to pool their benefit periods. Inflation protection is usually offered to the group policyholder, who can accept or reject it. Some groups offer only policies with future-purchase options, instead of built-in inflation protections. For an employer with offices in different states, GI affords more consistency in product and pricing across state lines.

From an enrollment standpoint, time is money. Therefore, typically, plan design is pre-selected by the employer, which avoids many of the rider and option issues that accompany individual products. Most carriers offer turnkey GI enrollment solutions. GLTCI enrollment only requires a signed group-enrollment form. Participants receive a certificate, and rate increases follow SIC code, as opposed to a statewide policy form. Some carriers require a minimum number of lives for GLTCI.

Combination Products

Combination product offerings deliver a product designed to serve two different risks and financial focuses. These products may be a good fit for certain segments of the worksite population, such as younger participants who want to cover multiple needs within a constrained budget. A combination life/LTCI or annuity/LTCI product may also attract individuals who question the value of "stand-alone" LTCI. These are the folks who ask, "What if I don't use it?" and worry that their premium dollars will be wasted.

LTCI benefits can be provided via riders to fixed, variable or equity-indexed plans from various product lines. Carriers have introduced a variety of LTCI rider designs attached to universal life insurance policies and annuities. There are also designs in which base plans may allow for a conversion or a guaranteed-insurability option for an LTCI product.

In all cases, it is imperative that advisors make clients aware that the combination product's LTCI coverage may not be as robust as the "stand-alone" policy and could fail to deliver the full protection they may need. Clients also need to be aware that using the LTCI benefit may reduce the available death benefit, have tax implications or impact annuity performance.

What do combination policies look like?

Combination policies can be a single-premium fixed annuity, which would accumulate assets from the general account to fund LTCI premiums and claims. They may also have a variable-annuity chassis, which would potentially generate cash values through sub-accounts to fund LTCI.

A cash-value life insurance policy (often universal life or variable universal life) provides a life insurance benefit. LTCI coverage is provided as a rider or as an acceleration of the death benefit. There are often options to increase the total sum paid beyond the initial death benefit of the life policy. For example, one company offers a rider that increases the amount of money available for long-term care to two times the death benefit of the life policy. Other products offer optional riders to extend long-term care benefits after the original death benefit has been depleted, for a specified period of time or for life. Still other products feature a residual death benefit that provides a limited death benefit, even if long-term care expenses exhaust the original face amount of the policy.

Some companies offer disability income (DI) policies with LTCI. Or, the DI policy may offer an exchange of the DI policy for an LTCI policy between the ages of 60 and 70, without evidence of insurability. Another variation involves offering a future purchase option that allows the insured to buy LTCI at some point in the future without evidence of insurability.

Tips

Before you offer LTCI at the worksite, consider the following eight tips:

1. Employer support is key.
2. Participation is higher when payroll deduction is offered.
3. Education and communication are essential when competing for benefits dollars. Unlike life insurance, which has one inevitable trigger common to all people, the need for LTCI may require some explanation.
4. To increase participation, tailor the plan to the motivation of each specific employee group, such as protecting retirement funds.
5. Product pricing is critical. Offer too many bells and whistles and you may find that only a very small percentage of the worksite population can afford the coverage.
6. Consider enrollment methodology and timing. Since it is new and different, offer LTCI during a separate enrollment, away from the core benefit cycle.
7. Offer current clients LTCI at the second or third enrollment, once "core" products are in place.
8. Combine different LTCI plan designs such as "stand-alone" plus UL/LTCI to capture more of the worksite population.

Keys to Good Case Selection

- A high concentration of well-educated and highly compensated individuals
- An employer with a track record of successful voluntary employee-benefits offerings
- A stable workforce or industry
- Employees with long tenures and/or an affinity to their employer (family-owned businesses can be particularly receptive)
- A large number of employees at each location
- Strong participation in flexible spending accounts (15 percent or greater)
- Strong participation in 401(k) plans (75 percent or greater)
- Strong participation in supplemental term life policies (40 percent or greater)

Motivating the Employer

In order for any company to remain competitive, it needs to customize benefits to meet its employees' changing life-stage needs. Employers have come to rely on employee-benefits insurance specialists, brokers and agents to make appropriate recommendations for how to best meet the needs of their workforce. It is important to recognize and communicate that LTCI has evolved into a flexible benefit that lends itself to worksite installation via numerous formats and in numerous combinations.

Pairing LTCI Designs

Each employee group requires an individual evaluation. Because one size may not fit all, LTCI offers many different plan designs.

Executive Carve-Out and Voluntary Plans

Companies may choose to make LTCI programs available to a select tier of employees. Employers may deduct premiums as an ordinary business expense, select employee participants based on their years of service, salary grade, job category, etc., and offer employer-paid long-term care plans to these specific tiers. Employer-paid premiums may be excluded from employee income. Consider adding a voluntary plan for the rank and file simultaneously or at the next enrollment.

Combine Combination and Stand-Alone LTCI Products

The "combo" LTCI plan paired with a "stand-alone" plan will appeal to a larger worksite population. There may be employees who will purchase a "combo" plan but may never purchase a "stand-alone" LTCI policy.

Combination plans might be well suited for those:

- Who are concerned with longevity and long-term care needs. The costs of long-term care services are rising at a rate that consistently outpaces inflation. A combination of an annuity and LTCI addresses the need for lifetime income as well as protection against long-term care costs, should the need arise.
- Who are concerned about outliving their assets, who want to maintain their independence and freedom of choice in care options and settings, and who are concerned about realizing the value of a stand-alone product.
- Who are addressing multiple needs within budget constraints.

Stand-Alone plans might be suited for those:

- Who reach an age at which it is impractical to purchase a large life insurance policy to create adequate long-term care protection, who do not have adequate or currently available funding, or who object to the charges imbedded in a combination product.
- Who have adequate life insurance. Life insurance addresses the issues of premature death and inheritance, but does nothing to protect the policyholder's present lifestyle. Stand-alone plans help address the need for affordable care. In the case of spouses or inheritance issues, it eliminates the potential for impoverishment.
- Who have assets they wish to protect. Of special interest are the partnership programs that most states offer, or are in the process of enacting, which are designed to help protect assets.
- Who want to obtain some protection against fluctuations in investment values and the timing of withdrawals.

An Employer/HR Agent Procedure Guide

Selling LTCI at the worksite involves two presentations: one is made to the employer or HR department and the second is made to the employees.

Voluntary benefits, especially in blue-collar cases, are price-sensitive, so when determining an LTCI offering, keep it simple and affordable.

Determine Program Basics

- Group size, minimum participation requirements, enrollment period, age ranges, salary ranges, underwriting concessions, applicable discounts, communication venues, website access, etc. Review these elements with the previous eight Tips in mind.
- Voluntary products that are currently in place. This will determine if a stand-alone or combination product is feasible.

Group Application Approval Form

- Create one of these forms if the carrier does not supply one. The form should include the agreed-upon enrollment period; type of underwriting concessions; age parameters; group type, agent, HR and billing contact information; re-enrollment underwriting concessions; frequency and expected dates; etc. It is best to have the employer or HR department sign off on this form.

Agent Tools

- A time table that indicates benchmarks, as well as who is responsible for meeting that benchmark. The employer or HR department should sign this document as well.
- An approved PowerPoint® presentation for a Webinar or Website
- A one-page cheat sheet with information particular to the enrollment or various state enrollments
- Survey/referral cards
- Approved thank-you letters
- Employer letter
- Annual "touch" letter for enrollees

Suggested Marketing Materials

Presentation folders, one for the employer's materials and one for the employees' handout that include your contact card.

Employer materials

- "Addressing the Need" brochure
  — 8 1/2 x 11" and/or tri-fold
- PowerPoint® presentation and/or flip chart
- Pre-approach letters to employers or benefit managers
- Follow-up letters to employers
- Mailer pieces with return cards
- Tax guide
- Sample email-blast announcements for employer approval
- Sample articles for employer newsletters
- Website link to the carrier's state-specific approved website for information and enrollment

Employee Materials. If you aren't using the carrier's standard materials, the items you have created should be pre-approved by the carrier.

- Product brochure
- "Addressing the Need" brochure
  — 8 1/2 x 11" and/or tri-fold

- Sample rate sheets
- Payroll stuffers
- Announcement letters/emails
- PowerPoint® presentations
- Posters and post cards
- Enrollment cover letter tailored to each group
- Reminder postcard/email and letter
- A one-page handout with websites and contact numbers for employees and spouses who do not attend a seminar or one-on-one meeting
- Announcement of website availability for information and enrollment
- "What to Expect Next" brochure that contains basic information for spouses so an employee does not have to be your salesperson.

HR and benefits managers will understand the broader appeal of the combination/stand-alone pairing. However, employers that have already completed successful life-insurance enrollments may prefer to use a stand-alone policy rather than disturb the current suite of product offerings. Ultimately, human resources departments, benefits advisors and employers need to consider their specific environment before deciding which approach is best for their employee population. The demand for LTCI makes it imperative that benefits advisors and agents become familiar with the available options. LTCI has come a long way in a short time and will continue to evolve into an extremely relevant benefit.

After years of study at the Sorbonne in Paris, **Carroll Golden** entered the professional world as an international translator. She continued her studies in Reims, France, and then took to the road, traveling to more than 64 countries, where she experienced many different ways of life. She later worked with a New York City law firm where she specialized in the translation of estate law. There, she gained valuable insights into how different customs and traditions influence governments and businesses.

Carroll has taught continuing-education classes and has authored numerous articles. She has specialized in group/worksite long-term care insurance and for several years contributed a monthly column about worksite long-term care insurance (LTCI) to *Benefits Selling* magazine. Carroll gained brokerage and field perspectives working with a national LTCI distributor and acquired home-office experience as director of business development for a national LTCI carrier.

Currently, Carroll is vice president of sales and marketing at Transamerica Life Insurance Company, LTCI Division located in Bedford, Texas, and is an active member of the Society of Financial Service Professionals, for which she previously served as the New Jersey chapter's president. She also served as chairperson for the Society of Actuaries Fifth Annual Intercompany LTCI Conference and currently serves on the board of directors of the Intercompany LTCI Association.

Carroll S. Golden
CLU, ChFC, CMFC, CLTC, LTCP, CASL, ALMI, ACS
Vice President Sales & Marketing
Transamerica Life Insurance Company
Long Term Care Division
1900 L. Don Dodson
Bedford, TX 76021
Phone: 817-285-3451
Cell: 817-709-6859
Fax: 817-285-3452
Email: cgolden@aegonusa.com

Chapter Ten

"Protected By The 10" The 10 Essential Elements of a Quality Limited Medical Program

JASON KROUSE
Chief Marketing Officer
Cost Containment Group

As legend has it, early in the 1980s, Charles Shoumaker, the former HR manager for convenience store chain Circle K, was busy trying to uncover a benefit package that would help reduce his massive turnover problem. Working in an industry with a very high turnover rate, Shoumaker was dedicated to finding a solution as he understood the direct correlation between offering a quality benefit package and turnover. He was searching for a benefit package, specifically a health care product, to meet the financial and lifestyle needs of his employee base. His search was fruitless because the risk he was looking to underwrite was outside the scope of the traditional carriers of that day. And so, Shoumaker decided to create a solution. The result was the development and introduction of the first limited medical plan.

The original limited medical plans had a very basic format: a few dollars per week covered about $1,000 of annual care. With such low benefit amounts and coverage limitations, the original plans were created to meet the needs of the bluest of the blue-collar industries. Because of the limitations of these first generation plans, the insurance industry shied away from the original low-cost, low-value limited benefit plans.

Today, because of the swelling number of uninsured and increases in plan benefits, the insurance industry has begun to embrace limited benefit plans as a viable alternative. This unprecedented growth of the uninsured, combined with marketplace acceptance of the plans, has resulted in exceptional profitability and growth for the insurance carriers that have entered the limited benefit marketplace. According to the 2006 annual sales survey conducted by Eastbridge Consulting Group, the total annual premium written in the voluntary medical line of business (limited medical plans, hospital indemnity and supplemental medical plans) is beginning to exceed the amount of annual premium written by more traditional worksite marketing products such as accident and cancer plans. This premium growth has enticed many new carriers to enter this profitable marketplace. Today, more than 50 percent of worksite carriers offer a hospital indemnity or limited medical plan, according to Eastbridge Consulting.

Such rapid growth has also caused marketplace confusion and uncertainty. While carriers, brokers, consultants and employers are accepting the reality that limited medical plans, when properly underwritten and implemented, do provide protection and value to the uninsured, the marketplace is struggling to understand and uncover the unknown limitations of the plans. Health care professionals are looking to the insurance industry to educate them about the limited medical plans, the benefits and inherent pitfalls.

Product Delivery

In order to best serve the clients' needs in uncovering a limited medical product with appropriate benefit levels, it is helpful to understand the companies involved in the delivery of the products and the roles they play.

1. Traditional worksite, accident/health and P&C carriers
   a. Many traditional carriers offer limited benefit plans through their regional distribution system.
   b. Some carriers offer products directly to employers.
   c. Some carriers utilize multiple touch points for coordination of benefits.
   d. Some carriers outsource customer service.
   e. Some carriers outsource fulfillment.
2. Traditional major medical insurance carriers
   a. A small but growing number of major medical carriers offer limited benefit plans through the brokerage community or through their direct sales forces.
   b. The majority of major medical carriers that have entered this market have done so via acquisitions.

c. Distribution is either direct to employers or via brokers/consultants.

d. Some carriers outsource fulfillment.

3. Limited medical managing general underwriters (LM MGU) and limited medical administrators
   a. A growing segment of the limited medical business
   b. Provide broker/consultant and employers with a turnkey process
   c. Many only work with one or two insurance carrier partners
   d. MGUs only distribute plans via brokers/consultants
   e. MGUs have created some very unique high-value products
4. Limited medical brokers
   a. Brokers who resell others' products and processes. The limited medical broker traditionally acts as a paid consultant for the brokerage community

Types of Limited Medical Plans:

Traditionally, the two major limited medical plans have been copay or indemnity plans. However, this line is becoming blurred as new hybrid copay/indemnity plans are being offered.

Indemnity Plan: Pays the provider or reimburses the insured a fixed amount for medical services rendered. It is important to review the specific policy language because if a procedure or event is not listed in the policy, the indemnity plan may not cover the medical service. This type of plan typically limits the number of services, visits, tests or days.

Copay Plan: Traditionally pays a percentage of a network discount price or usual, customary and reasonable (UCR) charges incurred. The provider submits the claim and the member is responsible for any applicable deductibles, copayments or coinsurance in excess of the benefit. It is important to be aware of annual maximums for outpatient and inpatient benefits. Some plans only pay above the copay to a limited dollar amount

Hybrid Copay/Indemnity Plans: The newest addition to this growing field, this next-generation product combines the benefits of indemnity and copay plans without many of the limitations inherent with the traditional copay plans.

It should be noted that many of all three types of these plans offer some type of continuation of coverage, whether as a COBRA-qualified plan or through member portability. All types of these plans can also be included in the client's Section 125 offerings.

Policyholders For Limited Medical Plans:

Group Plans: The policy is issued to the employer or group. When the policy is issued to an employer in an approved state, the majority of insurance carriers follow the situs rule, which is defined as: if the policy is issued to a group in an approved state for that carrier, then employees in all 50 states are eligible to enroll.

What to watch for:

- **A carrier not admitted in all 50 states.** Some carriers take the approach that if they are not admitted in a state, then the consumer must "self enroll" in those states, meaning that the employee must enroll without the assistance of an enroller.
- **A carrier that does not subscribe to the situs philosophy.** Some carriers only allow employees to enroll in states in which the plan has been officially admitted and approved. This is problematic when an employer's corporate offices are located in an approved state but some employees reside in non-approved states. For carriers that do not subscribe to the situs philosophy, employees in non-approved states are not eligible to enroll in the plan.
- **Pre-existing conditions or waiting periods.** For group plans, any pre-existing condition and/or waiting period should be waived. Possible exceptions include riders for pre-existing conditions for critical illness or disability parts of the plan.
- **Carriers that outsource various parts of the plan.** Many carriers take the risk and do very little else.
- **Savings for the employer.** Monthly employer and/or employee contribution rates should decrease if an employer is contributing to the cost of a plan.
- Many states require a minimum of 51 employees to be eligible in order to offer the plan.
- **State mandates.**

Who typically offers group plans:

- Employers with part-time, hourly or seasonal employees
- Employers that cannot afford to offer major medical insurance
    - This is the fastest growing group to offer these programs.
    - The majority of employers changing from a major medical plan will contribute to the monthly premium costs.

Specialty Plans: The growth of the underinsured marketplace has also resulted in the development of plans that fit the needs of some very important markets that traditionally have not offered medical plans.

Trucking: These plans offer benefits specific to the needs of truck drivers. Many of these plans are available for 1099 drivers, long-haul, short-haul, limousine, black car and taxi drivers. To determine if a particular group is covered, review the policy for limitations.

What to watch for:

- State availability
- Enrollment methods
- Cost
- Pre-existing condition exclusions or waiting periods.
- Additional ancillary benefits included in the plan
- Ability to collect premium via multiple methods including credit card and checking account withdrawal and settlement deduction.

Who typically offers this plan:

- Companies with 1099 workers
- Companies that do not offer major medical insurance

Staffing and Temp-To-Hire Agencies: Because of unpredictable work schedules, administration is the key to success. A carrier must be found that understands and is knowledgeable about missed premium deductions for these episodic workers. Staffing and temp-to-hire agencies traditionally require "first day" coverage.

What to watch for:

- Work with an organization that has experience in this market and ask for references.

- Pre-existing condition exclusions and waiting periods can be as long as 12 months. Closely examine the policy language.
- Many specialty staffing agencies, such as nurse staffing agencies, will contribute a percentage of the monthly cost.

Franchisees: The ability to cover franchisees without assigning a policy to the franchisor is essential to the success of this program. Work with an organization that offers and enrolls products that fit the needs of the franchise owner, managers and line workers.

What to watch for:

- State availability
- Additional product availability beyond limited medical such as short term disability, life insurance or critical illness
- Marketing plan. How will all levels of consumers be educated about the benefits of the plans?
- Enrollment method
- Pre-existing condition limitations and waiting periods
- Ask for references
- Rules regarding rate increases
- The ability to collect premium via credit card or checking account withdrawal.

10 Elements of a Quality Limited Medical Plan

While it is easy to spreadsheet a typical worksite or group product for which a carrier underwrites risk and occasionally pays claims, a limited medical plan has so many moving parts that are difficult to include in a spreadsheet. The following 10 elements will help uncover the hidden benefits and limitations of limited medical plans. This process will ultimately lead to a partner that can effectively meet the needs of your client.

1. Underwriting
2. The ability to incorporate multiple carriers into a single plan offering
3. Product review: the insurance benefits of limited medical plans
4. Providing true national PPO coverage

5. Discount medical provider organization statutes
6. Coordination of benefits/customer service
7. Marketing
8. Enrollment
9. Patient advocacy
10. Catastrophic care services

1. Underwriting
Reaction instead of innovation

Worksite carriers: The majority of carriers in this segment look to existing filings to meet the demands set by their marketing departments. Existing hospital indemnity plans and worksite accident products only partially meet the needs of the market and the pricing for many benefits in the plans do not match the associated risk. Carriers are limited to the additions and deletions they can make to the plans by the underlying policy. The majority of the worksite carriers offer indemnity plans only. Several carriers allow brokers to match and change benefits, but the majority require the broker to sell an existing canned plan.

Traditional group health carriers: Lacking the administrative process and underwriting knowledge, yet having vast financial resources, the major medical group health carriers that have entered this market have focused on the acquisition of existing limited medical administrators. While these acquisitions have brought instant and much-needed credibility to the limited medical marketplace, the slow process of merging cultures, sales forces and underwriting has not effected the change necessary to meet market demands. Many of the products available through this market still resemble the original products with low annual maximum benefits. However, changes are being made and benefit levels, service and administration is improving.

2. The ability to incorporate multiple carriers into a single plan offering

Limited Medical MGUs and administrators have the ability to combine the benefits of multiple carriers into one single superior product. This forward-thinking process has helped MGU and administrators develop products with well-rounded coverage and richer benefits. These new products incorporate benefits that focus on a member's medical needs.

The underwriting teams allow MGUs/administrators to weave together valuable sections of hospital indemnity policies with other high-value benefits. For example, if the underwriters determine that the plan requires a more robust emergency room benefit, they eliminate the hospital indemnity plan's base emergency room benefit and replace it with a stronger emergency room benefit. In addition, MGUs have the ability to include and expand benefits when a carrier cannot. The result is a plan with stronger benefits at an appropriate price.

3. Product review: the insurance benefits of limited medical plans

Doctor's office visits

Indemnity plans: The policy provides for a specific number of visits to a health care provider and the member is reimbursed a specific dollar amount between $25 and $150 per visit.

What to watch for: Make sure that the plan allows for assignment of the indemnity to the physician's office and the member is balance billed the difference. Also, ensure that the plan includes a minimum of three annual doctor office visits per family member. Finally, ensure the benefit covers both sickness and accident.

Copay plans: A true copay.

What to watch for:

- Many carriers consider the doctor's office copay an outpatient benefit. Outpatient benefits can include doctor's office visits, wellness benefits, emergency room visits, prescription benefits, diagnostics and labs and other outpatient benefits. Ultimately, the carrier will offer an annual outpatient maximum, sometimes as low as $1,000, with all claims for outpatient benefits counting toward that maximum. Ensure that the copay for the doctor's office visit is not included in an annual outpatient maximum.
- Outpatient physician office visits: Ensure that the visits are for both sickness and accidents.

Outpatient diagnostic test benefit

Indemnity plans: Pays the amount described in the plan for tests performed in an outpatient lab because of a covered sickness or injuries sustained in an accident. These plans pay for a certain number of tests at a defined reimbursement amount per test. These are generally billed separately from the doctor's office visit benefit.

Copay plans: Typically included in annual outpatient maximums. Check annual maximums to ensure members have enough coverage.

What to watch for:

- What tests are included? X-rays, lab tests, MRIs and CT scans should be covered. Sometimes, these are included in the outpatient maximum benefit.

Wellness visits

Indemnity plans: Reimburses the stated amount (typically between $25 and $150) for a visit to a health care provider when the member is neither sick nor injured.

What to watch for:

- Find out what tests are included in the wellness benefit. New plans are including Pap smears, mammograms and PSA tests.
- What is the annual benefit and how can the member utilize the benefit?

Copay plans: Typically included in the annual outpatient maximum. Check maximums and policy language for limitations.

Baby wellness

This is a great additional benefit that has been recently introduced. The benefit provides reimbursement for a set number of physician's office visits and tests from birth through 12 to 24 months. This is an important benefit that should be included in at least one of the plans offered.

Emergency room benefits

Indemnity plans: Pays a specified reimbursement amount for a specified number of visits to the emergency room.

What to watch for:

- Some indemnity plans include emergency room visits in the physician's office visit benefit. Emergency room visits should be offered as separate benefits.
- The emergency room benefit included in many plans only covers emergency room visits related to an accident and cannot be used for a sickness.

Copay plans: Emergency room visits typically count toward the annual outpatient maximum.

What to watch for:

- Become educated about what benefits and annual limits are included in the outpatient annual "bucket." If the average family visits the emergency room twice annually, be certain that the family still has a benefit available if and when they visit the physician's office and need blood work done.

Hospital admission

Indemnity plans: Reimburses the member a specified dollar amount upon the member's admission to a hospital.

What to watch for:

- Because the average hospital stay is four days or less, the hospital admission benefit is important.
- Many indemnity plans are per incident, offering benefits upon each hospital admission. Review the policy.

Copay plans: Typically part of the annual inpatient benefit.

What to watch for:

- Annual maximums

Daily in-hospital benefit

Indemnity plans: The benefit typically pays a certain dollar amount for a specified maximum number of days per incident if the member is confined in a hospital because of a covered accident or sickness.

What to watch for:

- It is important to check the annual or per-stay maximums of these plans. Typical plans pay for room and board. The benefit typically does not cover attending physicians or other visits by specialists. The benefit may not pay for pharmaceuticals administered in the hospital, so review the policy language.
- Some carriers pay this benefit in addition to the hospital admission benefit. If ICU is a covered benefit, is it paid in addition to the hospital confinement benefit?

Copay plans: Typically, an annual inpatient benefit is part of the plan.

What to watch for:

- Check the annual maximums. Read the policy to determine what is covered (pharmaceuticals, et cetera) under the inpatient benefits. Copay plans tend to offer a higher benefit level for shorter hospital stays.

In-hospital doctor's office visits

Indemnity and copay plans: Many plans do not offer this important coverage. While the plans provide reimbursements for room and board, they do not cover the costs of the attending physician or any specialists who visit the member in the hospital. Review the policy language to determine if this is covered under the plan.

Surgical schedules

Indemnity plans: In the majority of plans, if surgery is necessary because of an injury received in a covered accident or a covered sickness, the plan will pay for the surgical procedure up to the amount shown in the schedule of procedures and up to the maximum amount shown for each surgical procedure.

What to watch for:

- This can be a very confusing benefit. Review the schedule of procedures. Notice that the maximum stated in the proposal is typically the maximum allowed for the most expensive procedure. Many procedures in the schedule will only provide a reimbursement of a few hundred dollars, which does not offer much of a benefit.
- Try to find a company that offers 100 percent usual, customary and reasonable (UCR) instead of a schedule. This makes the maximum allowable a true maximum.
- Be careful that both in- and outpatient surgery is covered.

Copay plans: Varies by carrier, but can be included in the inpatient benefit maximum. Some do not provide surgical coverage. Review the policy language to understand what is really covered.

Anesthesia benefit

Indemnity plans: When a covered surgery is performed, the member will be reimbursed for between 25 and 75 percent of the amount paid under the surgery benefit.

What to watch for:

- If the member's plan offers a $500 surgery reimbursement and the anesthesia benefit provides a 25 percent reimbursement for the surgery, the member will be reimbursed $125 for anesthesia.

Copay plans: Typically lumped into the annual inpatient benefit. Review the policy for coverages and limitations.

Inpatient substance abuse

Utilization of this benefit is rather low. However, it has been priced affordably, so many add this to the plan to help increase coverage. The benefit is very limited in scope, so review the policy language.

Inpatient mental/nervous indemnity benefit

Utilization of this benefit is rather low. However, it has been priced affordably, so many add this to the plan to help increase coverage. The benefit is very limited in scope, so review the policy language.

Ambulance

This is an affordable benefit that should be included in every plan. It pays a reimbursed amount per ambulance trip. Some plans also include air ambulance if the user is located more than 50 miles from a facility.

Term life

This product must be guaranteed issue and require no medical exams or tests. The benefit amount is paid to the beneficiary in the event of the primary member's death.

What to watch for:

- The typical lower-priced limited medical plan will not included a term life benefit, but the mid- to high-end plans should include a minimum of $2,500 of term life insurance.
- The policy should provide coverage for the member's spouse and/or children if family coverage is selected.

Prescription drug benefit

When these plans were first introduced, prescription drugs were not as important as they are today. It is important to understand this part of the plan:

1. **Straight discount card**
   a. While these cards do offer savings for the member, they are typically very affordable and should only be included in entry-level plans.
   b. Only for those without health insurance.
2. **Tiered discount card**
   a. Formulary-based
   b. Plans offer a formulary that is divided into price tiers. Typically, the tiers are 10 percent, 20 percent, and 40 percent discount.
      1. Look for a company that incorporates technology into the plan offering.
         a. The key to a successful tiered plan is to be able to assist members in locating more affordable alternatives.
            1. These plans offer value if utilized correctly.
            2. Many of the generic drugs would be available at the same rate, regardless of the plan.
3. **Indemnity Rx benefits**
   a. Pays the stated amount per prescription filled with a specified number or prescriptions covered per year per member per family.
4. **Generic-only plans**
   a. Formulary-based
   b. Plans have either monthly or annual maximums. Ensure the maximums offer enough coverage.
   c. Can add $10 to $15 to the monthly single premium.
   d. The typical generic copay is $15.
5. **Brand and generic plans**
   a. Formulary-based
   b. Plans have either monthly or annual maximums. Ensure the maximums offer enough coverage.
   c. Can add $20 to $30 to the monthly single premium.
   d. The typical brand copay is $30.

6. **Free drug programs**

   Many pharmaceutical companies offer free drug programs to Americans whose earnings fall below a certain income threshold. Ensure that the limited medical partner has the ability to work with its members and enroll them in these valuable programs.

Critical illness

Pays the member the amount defined in the policy when the member is diagnosed with cancer, heart attack, stroke, major organ transplant or renal failure. Typically, a spouse will be covered at 50 percent of the benefit and children at 25 percent of the benefit amount.

What to watch for:

- To keep monthly premium amounts affordable, critical illness benefits are not included in many lower-priced plans.
- Carefully review the policy limitations to determine what is covered.
- Many of the included critical illness benefits come with pre-existing condition exclusions and waiting periods. Review the policy to determine this information.

Physical therapy

Indemnity plans: Pays for a specified number of visits for a specified reimbursement amount per visit. This benefit is not included in many plans.

Copay plans: Included in annual limits

Accident medical expense

If the member is injured in a covered accident and receives treatment from a physician within 365 days of the accident, the insurance company will pay the amount shown for actual expenses related to the accident. The typical policy will also cover any dental costs directly related to an accident.

What to watch for:

- This is a very important plan benefit. Be sure that a quality accident medical policy is wrapped into the limited benefit plan. Many carriers offer very limited accident policies or only offer a “light” version of the typical accident medical benefit, called a "sprain" or "broken-bone" benefit. Find a plan that offers an accident medical benefit that pays per incident with no annual or lifetime maximum on the number of accidents that are covered.

- A true accident medical expense benefit generally has much higher coverage limits when compared to a standard accident benefit.

AD&D

Pays the member or his beneficiary after an injury or accident that causes death or dismemberment within 365 days of the accident.

Sometimes, this benefit is only offered as a rider to a life policy. In that case, it may not cover spouse or dependents.

What to watch for:

- This is a very affordable addition to any plan. There is no reason to offer a plan without this affordable additional benefit.

4. Providing true national PPO coverage

One of the keys to ensuring that members achieve all of the savings incorporated in these plans and that the members' health care dollars are stretched as far as possible is the inclusion of a PPO network. While the majority of limited medical plans allow members to visit in- or out-of-network health care providers, consumers should visit an in-network provider to take advantage of the negotiated discounts whenever possible. PPO networks can offer savings of anywhere from 20 to 70 percent.

If the client has employees/members residing in multiple states, it is important to review the network coverage of the PPO being offered as the majority of PPOs do not offer true national coverage, regardless of their size. All PPOs have coverage holes and one must be able to locate those gaps.

An important fact to understand is that the majority of PPOs present participating physicians' contracts in a multiple of network options. Physicians can typically choose between straight discount networks, limited medical networks, HMOs, PPOs or other networks. Thus, even though the name of the network is easily recognizable, be sure that the network with the highest savings is included.

Another important element of the PPO is the saving percentages for which the physicians have contracted. Savings can range from as low as 10 to over 60 percent, so it is important to include a network with as high a level of savings as possible.

Worksite carriers: Initially, many carriers did not offer a PPO network as a plan benefit. Today, the majority of carriers offer a PPO as part of the plan. However, several carriers still do not mandate that a PPO be included and some even require the consumer to pay an additional amount for the inclusion of the PPO plan. Check to ensure that a PPO is included with the core plan and that the PPO has coverage in the applicable states and regions.

Health carriers: These carriers have incorporated their nationally known brand name PPOs in their limited medical plans. These PPO networks offer strong savings and excellent coverage.

What To Watch For: Providers contracted with major medical carriers which now offer limited medical products are unfamiliar with the increased risk of being unable to collect on claims which are not covered by the plan.

Limited medical MGUs/administrators: Traditionally, these entities include PPO networks into their plans. Review coverage of the PPO networks. A few MGUs/administrators have merged multiple PPOs to create a true national PPO. This is very important for large multi-state clients.

5. Discount medical provider organization statutes

Today, at least 21 states have discount medical provider organization (DMPO) statutes. These statutes provide direction and governance to non-insurance health-related networks. While the intent of these statutes was honorable, many states took their governing powers to the extreme and created an environment of overreaching regulations and requirements, leaving the consumer more vulnerable than ever.

The true value of DMPO benefits is the additional savings and enhanced benefits that can be added to a limited medical plan for a very affordable price. For example, discount prescription drug plans, dental networks, vision networks, hearing care, employee assistance programs, wellness, chiropractic, holistic care, diabetic supplies, nurse hotlines and other health care-related programs that offer true value and deep savings can be included in limited medical plans.

Worksite carriers: Many original versions offered upgraded hospital indemnity benefits without the additional savings of DMPO networks. Today, the majority of worksite carriers partner with DMPOs that manage this portion of the limited medical plan.

What to watch for:

- Be aware of the coordination of benefits, which should be simple.

Major medical carriers: Traditionally, the major medical carriers have not filed their products with core DMPO benefits.

What to watch for:

- The majority of major medical carriers charge additional monthly fees for dental, vision, hearing and other DMPO benefits.

Limited medical MGUs/administrators: There are two camps. The first partners with DMPOs and do not hold their own DMPO licenses while the second is an administrator that holds their own DMPO approvals.

What to watch for:

- Coordination of benefits

6. Coordination of benefits/customer service

The ability to coordinate all of the insurance benefits and DMPO networks in a single plan is the key to a quality health care experience for the end user.

Worksite carriers:

- Does the member have a single toll-free number to call for customer service for all insurance-related and DMPO benefits?
- Can the indemnity benefit be assigned to the medical provider and the member balance-billed for the remaining portion?

Major medical carriers:

- What DMPO benefits do they include in the core plan?

Limited medical MGU/administrators:

- Does the member have a single toll-free number to call for customer service for all insurance-related and DMPO benefits?
- If a product that incorporates benefits from multiple insurance carriers is offered, how are the benefits coordinated?
- If the MGU/administrator does not hold a DMPO license, who provides customer service and how?
- Who coordinates the savings for these benefits?

7. Marketing

Professional marketing materials are imperative from an education, enrollment and compliance standpoint. Work with organizations that have internal marketing departments. This will allow for much greater control of the development and delivery of this important function.

Marketing materials include: Pre-enrollment letters, enrollment brochures, posters, paycheck stuffers, postcards, educational CDs and question-and-answer sheets. The enrollment materials must clearly explain that limited medical plans are not major medical insurance and are not designed as a substitute for such. These compliance issues must be balanced with the need to educate the consumers about the benefits and savings offered by the plan. Full disclosure of the limitations of the plan must be offered.

Worksite carriers: The marketing assistance available from carriers varies, so check with the carrier. Many carriers provide sample materials for review and require agents/brokers/consultants to do all of the printing and distribution of the materials.

Major medical carriers: Enrollment support varies by carrier. Check with the carrier's representative about the breadth of assistance available.

Limited medical administrators/MGUs: Determine if the MGU/administrator outsources the marketing function. If the MGU/administrator does not, then there will be additional control of this important step. In addition, keeping this function in-house is traditionally more affordable.

Typically, the MGUs/administrators provide complete turnkey marketing support. They design, develop, print and mail all marketing materials. If the product has been priced correctly, then this service should already be priced into the plan.

8. Enrollment

The enrollment process is extremely important to the client. Working with an organization that controls the enrollment process from beginning to end is critical. In addition, working with an organization that does not pay commissions to those enrolling the limited medical plans is paramount, as enrollers should take a more consultative approach when enrolling employees into these plans.

Worksite carriers: Traditionally, carriers leave the enrollment process to the broker. Occasionally, the carrier will partner with an enrollment company that will split the commission with the broker to handle the enrollment.

Major medical carriers: These carriers tend to work in conjunction with agents/brokers.

Limited medical MGU/administrators: In-house enrollment centers: Many MGU/administrators own and operate internal enrollment centers. This extends control over the entire process. If the MGU/administrator does not own and operate an internal center, it is important to understand which organization will be handling the enrollment process, how the enrollers will be compensated and how the process works.

- Make sure the call center is located within the confines of the MGU's/administrator's office.
- Ensure that the enrollers are W2 employees and that 1099 contractors are only employed on rare occasions.
- Review the script the enrollers will use. This will allow for analysis of the sales philosophy incorporated in the enrollment center. Look for a script that helps guide a member to the product that best fits his needs.

Billing administration: Many clients need alternative billing options. Look for a partner that also has the ability to collect premiums via credit card or checking account withdrawals in addition to payroll deduction.

9. Patient advocacy

Limited medical plans offer many employees their first health care experience. It is imperative that members have a stress-free experience. The selected limited benefit partner should have a patient advocacy department with a toll-free number available to members. The primary focus of the patient advocacy department is to help members understand the benefits of the plan while maximizing their savings. The patient advocacy function should be separate from the customer service function.

10. Catastrophic care/catastrophic services

Limited benefit plans do not cover catastrophic events or illnesses. However, the reality is that members with limited benefit plans do experience catastrophic events. Thus, it is important that the chosen organization have a service team to deal with these events. They might arrange an operation overseas or work with the Lance Armstrong Foundation on behalf of a member who has cancer or locate a therapist to help guide the member through this difficult time. It is important that the selected partner offers this type of service.

What does the future hold?

After some uncertain times, the marketplace has accepted limited benefit plans as a viable health care option. Already, attempts are underway to underwrite, price and coordinate limited benefit plans with catastrophic plans. In addition, low-limit benefit plans that coordinate with high-deductible major medical plans are also in a growth stage and are in high demand.

As the health care dilemma continues, the insurance industry will be asked to create new plans that offer value, savings and coverage for all who are in need.

Jason Krouse received his Juris Doctor degree from Nova Southern Shepard Broad Law Center in 1997. During law school, Jason co-founded the Legal Club of America, a national discounted legal referral company, for which he served as executive vice president until he was appointed its director in 1998.

After leaving Legal Club of America, Jason served as the executive vice president and senior vice president of sales of National Accident Insurance Underwriters (NAIU) and National Accident Insurance Consultants (NAIC). Along with other senior NAIU and NAIC executives, Jason purchased the assets of the organization and merged the company with United Health Programs of America and Patriot Health and created Cost Containment Group, a holding company with a focus on controlling costs in the health care and special risk accident market. Jason currently serves as the chief marketing officer of Cost Containment Group (CCG) where he oversees the sales and marketing for United Health Programs of America, Patriot Health and Ocean Consulting Group.

Jason is a past president of the Mass Marketing Insurance Institute (MI2) and sits on the board of directors of the Benefit Marketing Association (formerly NAPES) He resides in Parkland, Florida with his wife Nicole, son Zachary and daughter Jadyn.

Jason Krouse
Chief Marketing Officer
Cost Containment Group
1 Eileen Way
Syosset, NY 11791
Phone: 516- 576- 9264
Fax: 516-576-9268
Email: Jason@ccgfamily.com
Website: www.ccgfamily.com

Chapter Eleven

Wellness At Work

MARIE J. KILLIAN, J.D.
IHPM Practice Leader
Trion

I. What is Wellness? Why the Need for Wellness at Work?

Personal wellness is the condition of good physical and mental health maintained by proper diet, exercise and lifestyle habits. It is an active process that requires taking responsibility for one's own health while maintaining a balance among various facets of life activities. The result is a state of optimal well-being, not simply the absence of illness. Wellness management emphasizes the importance of engaging in efforts to be as healthy as possible as it applies to the areas of physical, mental, emotional and spiritual well-being.

A comprehensive wellness program at work is one that assists employees in improving health, is sponsored by the employer, involves all employees and may be extended to family members. Such a program provides an opportunity to voluntarily make behavior changes that reduce health and injury risks, improve skills as health care consumers and enhance overall well-being, function and productivity. Worksite health-promotion programs emerged in the 1970s and have evolved from a unique new benefit offered by a few employers to a standard business practice offered by employers of all sizes in every type of industry.

Today there are many good reasons for employers to address wellness at work. In a constantly changing, highly competitive global marketplace, keeping workers healthy and productive is not only good business, but smart business. Because wellness and health are key components of corporate responsibility reports and "best places to work" rankings, corporate success is increasingly linked to the health of workers.

Many employers consider their employees to be an important, if not the most important, asset. Wellness is therefore an investment in human capital. Employees are more likely to be on the job and performing at their highest levels when they are in optimal physical and psychological health.

The worksite is increasingly being recognized as a great place to implement health and wellness strategies. Indeed, worksites are proven to be the single most important channel through which to systematically reach this country's adult population.

The employee base forms a large population to target, with more than 60 percent of American adults working, and 82 percent of the U.S. population linked in some way to a worksite. The sedentary nature of the service sector increases employees' risk of chronic disease, and today many more employees work within the service sector than in previous decades. Working adults spend more time at work than in any other setting, with many spending 2,000 or more hours per year—or at least one-third of each week day—at work. Therefore, providing worksite health programs is an efficient way to reach a substantial number of people, especially when the programs are expanded to include employees' family members.

Typically, the attempts of group health plans to succeed in illness prevention and disease management are challenged because their "membership" turns over, on average, every 18 months. However, employers who retain employees for substantially longer periods of time are motivated to invest in their health and productivity and therefore are particularly motivated to invest in wellness programs.

Employers are also increasingly faced with the challenges that accompany an aging workforce. Medical costs increase by an estimated 25 percent between the ages of 40 and 50 and increase by 35 percent between the ages of 50 and 60. Employers recognize the need to retain their experienced workers as they age, but productive and cost-effective aging is dependent upon healthy aging.

Interestingly, while age is certainly a factor in increased medical costs, it is less significant than the presence of health risks such as smoking, obesity, lack of exercise and diabetes, which impact every age group. At least one quarter of all health care costs incurred by working adults can be attributed to modifiable health risks such as diet, exercise, tobacco use and stress. Additionally 50 percent to 70 percent of all diseases are preventable, as they are associated with modifiable health risks.

Finally, wellness programs offered at work provide benefits for both employees and employers.

Employees benefit in the following ways:

- Improved quality of life achieved by reduced health risk factors
- Increased knowledge about the relationship between lifestyle and health
- Increased opportunity to take control of their health and medical treatment
- Increased morale resulting from the perception of the employer's interest in their health and well-being
- Reduced work absences
- Reduced medical costs
- Reduced pain and suffering from illness and accidents

Employers benefit in the following ways:

- Increased employee morale and loyalty
- Improved corporate image
- Increased worker productivity
- Health care-cost conscious workforce
- Enhanced recruitment messaging
- Improved retention of employees

Cost savings achieved by:

- Decreased health care utilization
- More appropriate use of health care
- Reduced disability claims
- Reduced sick leave and absenteeism
- Reduced premature retirement for health reasons
- Fewer jobsite accidents
- Lower casualty insurance costs

Workplace wellness programs can benefit businesses of every size. Statistically, even in a company of only 100 people, an employer will typically encounter the following risk factors:

- 60 are not getting sufficient exercise
- 50 don't wear their seat belts regularly and are a safety risk
- 50 feel they're under moderate stress
- 35 are overweight by 20 percent or more and that statistic is increasing rapidly
- 30 use tobacco products
- 27 have cardiovascular disease
- 25 have high cholesterol
- 10 drink alcohol at an excessive level
- 10 have high blood pressure
- 5 have diagnosed diabetes
- 5 have undiagnosed diabetes

II. How to Get Started – Best Practices

There is no one-size-fits-all wellness program. A program may include a wide variety of services, educational material and support designed to improve employee health. Regardless of the nature of the interventions selected, a wellness program should have the following "Best Practice" components:

- Secure the support of senior management. Create a wellness champion among senior management. One of the most important indicators of the success of a wellness program is the visible support of senior management. It is essential that leaders support health as an important value in the organization. Senior management can support wellness in many different ways: by providing input during the planning process; approving funding; demonstrating leadership by becoming personally involved; and permitting flexible schedules to accommodate wellness activities.
- Create a wellness committee or team. The focus of the wellness committee is to plan, promote and implement the program. The committee should be composed of a cross section of employees representing various occupations and departments within

the organization. It should include top management, union representatives, human resources, health and safety departments, information technology and employees interested in health and wellness. An active and engaged wellness committee helps to create a sense of employee ownership in the program.

- Base the program upon a needs assessment and data. Consider the needs, interests and expectations of the participants. Obtain information through formal surveys, employee feedback and group discussions. Invite comments, suggestions and recommendations from employees. Employees are more willing to participate and support wellness efforts if they are involved in the decision-making process. Assess existing demographic data, health care costs, sick leaves and disability absences, workers compensation experience and turnover rates. Low turnover rates are a significant indicator of the success of a wellness program. Consider what has been done in the past for health promotion, what worked and what did not.
- Create a customized operating plan. Establish a mission statement and goals for the wellness program. Set timelines and assign responsibilities. The mission statement for the wellness program should closely align with the corporate mission statement. Generally a primary goal is to improve the health and well-being of employees and their family members. Brand the program with a unique name and then communicate it to employees.

When the support of senior management, mission statement and committee are in place, the next step is to select service providers and the interventions desired. Best-practice programs typically include a health screening (usually a health-risk assessment), incentives to encourage participation in the programs, health counseling or coaching, health-improvement programs, and worksite-wide activities.

Ideally, a health-risk assessment is administered to every employee on an annual basis. It is an online tool or paper questionnaire that examines an employee's health status, risk factors, family history and lifestyle. It shows employees where there is a need to improve in terms of health, personal relationships and work performance. Health-risk assessments can be used as a stand-alone tool but are much more effective when integrated into a well-developed wellness program. Typically, upon completion of the assessment, a report is generated for the employee detailing his or her specific health risks and needs. This report can serve as a road map to direct the employee to available programs, which may include health education via web site tools, nurse advice lines, self-care books, newsletters, workbooks, health fairs, fitness centers and seminars.

The health-risk assessment is often used in conjunction with biometric testing which generally includes measurements of blood pressure, height, weight, body mass index, and a finger-stick blood draw to test blood glucose and cholesterol. It may also include additional blood screens, flexibility and strength testing, prostate cancer screening, bone scans and mammograms.

Well-designed incentive programs can significantly contribute to a wellness program's success. Incentives are typically offered to increase participation rates, to help with completion of or attendance at programs, and to encourage individuals to adopt and/or maintain healthy behaviors. Successful incentive programs are based upon achieving goals that are attainable by most individuals and should be designed with the employer's culture and population in mind. After all, what is considered an incentive in one work environment may not be of interest to another group of employees. Incentives may include a variety of rewards such as, t-shirts, gift cards, fitness books and reductions in health-insurance premium contributions.

When a reward in a wellness program is contingent upon satisfying a health-related factor, the Health Insurance Portability and Accountability Act's (HIPAA) non-discrimination requirements must be met. They include the following: the reward or incentive cannot exceed 20 percent of the total cost of single employee coverage; the program must be "reasonably designed" to promote health or prevent disease; qualifying individuals must be allowed to participate in the same incentives program each year; alternative methods for obtaining the reward must be made available; and all plan materials describing the program must disclose the availability of a reasonable alternative method.

An increasingly popular targeted intervention in best-practice programs is health coaching, which may be either telephonic or administered at the worksite. A health coach will contact or be contacted by the employee and provide support and education to reduce selected health risks. The number of phone calls or visits at the worksite is usually contingent upon the number of risk factors an employee has and whether he or she is considered low, moderate or high risk.

Specific interventions for individuals may also include weight-loss programs, nutrition counseling, exercise programs, participation in fitness centers, smoking- or tobacco use- cessation programs, and stress management.

Finally, worksite-wide activities are developed that are available to all employees and are often group activities. These may include health fairs, walking clubs, smoke-out programs, aerobic exercise sessions, men's health discussion groups, women's health discussion groups, sports leagues, fun runs, corporate competitions, nutritional potluck meals and mentoring systems. The "Best Practice" employer will offer the program on an ongoing basis rather than limiting it to one-time events.

III. Return on Investment (ROI) Expectations

Before employers are able to control health care costs, they must first improve the health of their employees. Healthy employees are more productive, use fewer health care services and enjoy a higher morale. A significant portion of the average company's health care costs is related to the lifestyles of its employees. The total cost associated with improving lifestyle risks through wellness programs varies greatly depending upon the program components selected as well as the intensity, duration and level of incentives offered.

Numerous studies of worksite wellness programs have demonstrated that business returns come over a period of time and are usually not realized until at least the second year of the program. According to the *American Journal of Health Promotion*, employers can expect a 3-to-1 return on every dollar spent on wellness. The *Journal* studied the plans of 200 companies and saw an average of a 3.5-to-1 return over three to six years. Variations in ROIs result from program design, wellness programs implemented and the overall state of the employees' health at the start of the programs.

Studies have shown reductions in health care costs ranging from 7 percent to 60 percent. Reductions in specific risk factors result in medical claims savings. For example, the annual health care cost for tobacco users is, on average, $1,200 to $6,000 higher than for non-tobacco users. Decreasing the number of smokers in the workplace can save an employer tens or hundreds of thousands of dollars annually, not to mention the direct savings enjoyed by employees who are no longer purchasing tobacco products.

Health care costs for obese workers are 35 percent higher than for average-weight workers. The average absenteeism cost for workers identified as obese was almost $900 greater annually than for employees who have a normal body-mass index. A sustained reduction of just 10 percent in body weight yields significant health and economic benefits.

What's more, reducing obesity in the workplace also reduces disability and absence costs.

The cost effectiveness of a wellness program should be evaluated and monitored on an on-going basis but the direct cost savings is only one of the returns realized from a wellness program. In addition to the medical cost savings, measurable savings have been shown in other areas. Studies have found reductions in sick leaves ranging from 12 percent to 68 percent, and decreased workers compensation costs ranging from 20 percent to 52 percent.

While many studies demonstrate compelling business reasons for wellness programs, reducing costs is only one objective. The bottom line is about people—enhanced morale, higher employee job satisfaction, decreased turnover, reduced absenteeism and decreased presenteeism, which means being at work but lacking focus or productivity because of a health condition.

IV. The Next Phase – Integrated Health and Productivity Management

As the wellness at work movement develops and employers succeed in managing medical costs, progressive companies will move toward extending health management to include absence and productivity management and improvement. This process begins by assessing and aligning all health-related activities with disability and absence programs, but it all starts with wellness.

Connecting wellness interventions to other worksite services and vendors, such as disease management, employee-assistance programs, disability plans, workers compensation, absence management, and family and medical leave acts is the foundation for Integrated Health and Productivity Management. The strategic approach to Integrated Health and Productivity Management is similar to the development of wellness programs and results in direct and indirect cost savings to employers and numerous benefits to employees.

Today, employers have many options and decisions to make regarding the development of health management and productivity programs, but wellness at work programs are more business-relevant than ever. In addition to fulfilling a business need, wellness at work programs improve the quality of life that employees enjoy at work, at home and in their communities.

Marie Killian is the Integrated Health and Productivity Management Practice Leader at Trion. She is responsible for developing strategies that integrate data and services across the areas of health, absence, disability and organizational health.

With more than 20 years of experience with long-term and short-term disability, workers compensation, absence management, and the Family and Medical Leave Act (since its enactment), Marie works to help employers create strategies that balance employer, employee and financial outcomes.

Prior to joining Trion, Marie spent 13 years as a vice president at Aon Consulting, where she provided consulting services for integrated disability and benefits management to Fortune 500 employers. She also developed the Workers Compensation Rehabilitation Department for Harleysville Insurance Company, served as a risk manager for a multihospital system, and has practiced law with a Philadelphia law firm.

A graduate of Temple University Law School, Marie earned her Juris Doctor degree and served as an editor of the Temple Law Review. She has been a speaker at Risk and Insurance Management Society (RIMS) conferences on the topics of absence management and integrated disability and has taught Certified Employee Business Specialist (CEBS) Program courses.

Marie J. Killian, J.D.
IHPM Practice Leader
Trion
2300 Renaissance Boulevard
King of Prussia, PA 19406
Business phone: 610-684-3270
Mobile phone: 610-420-8265
Email: mkillian@trion.com
Website: www.trion.com

CHAPTER TWELVE

Legal Plans: A Critical Component of the Employee Benefits Package

ROBERT L. HESTON, JR.
PRESIDENT AND CEO
LEGAL ACCESS PLANS, L.L.C.

Legal plans are one of the most popular value-added employee benefit programs. The desirability of these plans as a voluntary employee benefit has been increasing exponentially in the last few years. According to research conducted by the National Resource for the Consumers of Legal Services, the total number of Americans purchasing legal service plans is expected to increase from approximately 6 million in 1990 to more than 68 million by 2015. Several consulting firms estimate that by the end of the decade, more than 35 percent of American companies will offer a legal service plan to employees.

Today's credit crunch means that millions of Americans are literally a lawsuit away from being financially wiped out. Each day, thousands of Americans are dragged into court to defend themselves from lawsuits. And each day, thousands of Americans file lawsuits. For employees, the threat of a lawsuit has never been greater.

Costly Misconceptions

The increase in the number of Americans faced with legal problems has created the widespread belief that access to lawyers and legal advice is more necessary than ever. At the same time, however, a growing number of employees feel disconnected from the legal system, and most believe that lawyers are inaccessible and too expensive.

When asked about their preparedness for a legal situation, most employees respond, "I do not have my own lawyer," or "I do not know a lawyer to call in a legal emergency." As a result, countless employees forego legal services until the last possible minute or, in some cases, until they have absolutely no other choice. It is not uncommon for Americans served with a lawsuit to simply ignore it. When asked why they failed to respond to the lawsuit or speak with an attorney, some common answers include:

- "I did not do anything wrong so they can't get me for anything."
- "I did not know a lawyer who I could call for help."
- "I did not know what kind of lawyer I needed."
- "The plaintiff is wrong, so I did not feel I needed to respond."
- "I cannot possibly afford a lawyer's fees."

As a result, thousands of dollars in liens, judgments, bankruptcies, repossessions, collections, foreclosures and credit restoration must be spent to undo the damage caused by the simple delay in responding to a lawsuit.

Crucial Coverage

Today's average working American family is significantly affected by legal problems. Approximately 43 percent of the legal problems that American employees experience involve family law. Divorce, separation, child custody, child support, visitation, divorce decree modifications, adoptions, and hundreds of other related legal problems are the most common. A company considering a legal plan should analyze the plan for its divorce and family law coverage and eliminate any potential plan that does not include this area of law as a "core" coverage, as the need for family law coverage will assuredly be significant.

A Growing Demand for Legal Plans

Employees in need of legal help are requesting legal plans as an employee benefit and employers are responding. Today, most companies offer legal plans on a voluntary, 100-percent employee-paid platform.

HR managers and employers find that the right legal plans can:

- Serve as a key component of a retention benefits strategy
- Increase productivity by helping employees handle legal problems quickly and effectively

- Reduce employees' emotional distress by providing needed legal counseling
- Offer a built-in mediation benefit for work-related conflicts between employees
- Present employers and employees with an inexpensive product relative to the value it provides, resulting in an attractive return on investment

Understanding Legal Service Providers and Plans

Legal plans range from those that provide basic benefits to those that offer comprehensive insurance coverage. Legal plans are typically offered in group/worksite environments, including large corporations, associations, small companies, financial institutions, unions and other affinity groups.

Legal plans are being sold by worksite insurance producers and brokers in record numbers, as well as by marketing companies, direct marketers, financial institutions and affinity marketers. Legal plans are marketed to corporations and organizations through either an employer-paid or a voluntary benefit services platform, although in the worksite market, the voluntary benefit is currently the most popular offering. While a few of the largest corporations and public entities may not encourage a broker relationship, most companies, public entities, financial institutions and associations offer legal plans as employee benefits that can be sold through insurance agents and producers.

Legal plans are usually grouped by coverage type and consist of the following three plans:

1. Indemnity Plans
2. Access or Managed Plans
3. Discount or Referral Services

Indemnity Plans

Indemnity plans are commonly thought of as insurance plans, similar in coverage and benefits to dental or vision plans, and include complete claims administration service. Employees submit claims supported by paid bills from providers, or payments can be made directly to the provider attorneys. There are specified covered benefits with specific limitations, and, depending upon the plan, there can be deductibles and waiting periods as well.

Legal indemnity plans typically cover specified services defined in a policy, summary plan document or plan booklet, up to a certain maximum coverage. For example, a legal plan may cover a motor vehicle license suspension representation up to a total amount of $750. This means the plan will pay the attorney representing the member a fee of $750 and the attorney can charge the member for any additional amount.

Along with these maximum coverages, a legal plan may also provide certain services to employees or their dependents at no charge. Free consultations are often provided, which allow employees to ascertain the nature of a legal problem without incurring legal fees. In this way, the legal plan can help an employee prevent a legal problem by providing resources and services that enable that employee to learn about the potential risks of a perceived legal threat and decide whether to pursue, settle, or ignore the legal matter.

Other benefits that may be provided at no charge or at a discounted rate are specified in the plan and may include document reviews, living wills, simple wills, complex wills, dispute-resolution letters and phone calls, as well as a designated number of hours of legal assistance for matters such as governmental agency disputes or small-claims court problems.

Access or Managed Legal Plans

Another popular type of legal plan offered in the worksite marketplace is the access plan. This legal plan typically covers specific legal benefits and services fully or at discounted rates. Under most access plans, however, there is no insurance or reimbursement and the plan member is ultimately liable for all legal expenses.

There are several reasons why an access plan is attractive to a large percentage of employees:

1. Administration and customer service, credentialing methodologies and complaint- and problem-resolution services are sophisticated and streamlined
2. The level of preventive help available with some plans is significant
3. The access plan is usually more affordable than the indemnity plan
4. The access plan meets the needs of nearly 92 percent of employees without costing them any out-of-pocket expense

Discount Legal Plans or Referral Services

Discount legal plans usually offer a minimal number of legal benefits and have a scaled-down administration infrastructure. In fact, the infrastructure of many of these plans is merely a toll-free phone number that a member can call to access the stated services for an initial consultation.

Choosing the Right Legal Plan

To address the most basic needs of employees involved in a legal problem, a legal plan must offer an effective delivery system that accomplishes the following: (1) promotes and facilitates easy access to network provider attorneys; and (2) offers access in a manner that will overcome any fears or concerns plan members may have about contacting and working with attorneys.

Questions to ask when selecting a legal plan:

- How many attorneys are in the network?
- What are the benefits and how do they compare with those of other plans?
- What are the limitations and exclusions?
- What Internet resources are available?
- What extra services are available?

The following operational and service questions will help HR managers and worksite producers select the right legal plan for their employees:

1. *How does the plan select its lawyers and how does it demonstrate that quality lawyers are selected?* [While the legal plan must have a large and developed network of attorneys, the legal plan with the largest number of lawyers is not always the best legal plan]
2. *How does the legal plan measure the quality of service offered? By what specific measures can a legal plan administrator demonstrate quality rendered by the law firm providers?*
3. *What type of proprietary, secure and encrypted technology platform is used to administer and integrate all of the legal plan service delivery functions?*
4. *What infrastructure is in place that offers personalized assistance for employees who may not know how to navigate the legal system or work with attorneys?*

5. *What system is used to ensure that employees have the best attorney to handle their particular legal matter?*

What to look for in a legal plan company

A legal plan provider should be selected for its experience, track record and integrity.

1. Look for legal plan companies that have been in business for several decades. The legal plan field may be new to insurance producers, but the best legal plans' networks of attorneys have been built over three or four decades.
2. There are no A.M. Best's or Moody's ratings for legal plans unless the plan company offers insurance products as well, so check into the company's ownership and principals to help determine how the business is run. If it is a public company, check the stock prices for recent trends in sales, revenues and earnings.
3. Find legal plans that not only operate in the worksite industry, but also have well-developed divisions and operations in other industries that give the organization some breadth and economy of scale.
4. Find companies with several years of real legal plan experience.
5. Find a legal plan that offers access plans and indemnity or fully insured plans, as your clients have many different needs and goals. Some may want a less expensive access plan, while others may want to offer employees a complete array of benefits with a fully insured plan.

Critical Components of a Legal Plan

When it comes to evaluating a legal plan, the most critical questions are those that examine the attorney network. How has it been built and how is it administered? An effective legal plan should offer the following:

- More than 25 years of experience as a legal plan administrator, and not just operations in another insurance field
- A provider network that does not use the same network attorneys as other less quality-driven legal plans
- A minimum daily level of legal referrals made to provider law firms (this will illustrate how developed the plan's operations are)
- Proven stringent credentialing requirements
- Strict adherence to attorney-client privilege principles in all communications

- A developed law-firm model that dictates network recruitment goals
- A service delivery method that promotes ease of access, not just a system that looks like other insurance programs
- A proven track record of satisfied clients who can provide their own independent satisfaction reports about the legal plan their employees' use

Why Should Legal Plans Be an Integral Part of Your Worksite Benefits Insurance Practice?

Many insurance agents realize that the worksite market is where the "benefits action" is right now. Yet many agents still think they need to focus their efforts on "core" or traditional insurance products and don't see the need to sell non-insurance products. Some have become converts by learning the hard way when their best clients find a new insurance producer who integrates traditional insurance products with one or more non-traditional products – perhaps a legal plan. Producers with long-standing relationships who are not worried about losing business to other agents may end up looking over their shoulders at a new competitor who just brought in a legal plan and now has an entree into the company that may need other insurance products as well.

Producers often overlook the connection between legal plans and life or disability sales. The simple-wills portion of many legal plans can be used to raise the issue of preparing for the future. The need for a will supports the discussion of life insurance.

Additionally, the fact that legal emergencies usually arise without warning supports the discussion of a disability or cancer policy. And the statistic that 38 percent of employees are caught in the "sandwich" generation – caring for their children and their elderly parents – can help illustrate the need for a long-term care policy.

Legal Plans as a "Door-Opener"

Employers often tire of hearing the same pitch about the same "core" products. Talking about non-traditional worksite products like legal plans can be an excellent way to attract the attention of a busy corporate manager. And, since legal plans provide substantial benefits to employees at no out-of-pocket cost to the employer, producers who offer such plans don't just get a foot in the door; they also solidify client relationships and set themselves apart from other brokers who have not yet adapted any new product strategies.

Benefits such as legal plans that are not salary or bonus related can also be effective tools for employee retention and recruitment. After all, these benefits allow the employer to offer products and services that most employees would not be able to purchase on their own.

Conclusion

Worksite producers seeking a new worksite product, high revenue-share opportunities, value-added programs for employees, and a program that will offer their client companies a high return on investment, should consider adding the right legal plan to their worksite portfolio.

Legal plans come in many forms, so to choose the most appropriate plan, producers should examine the infrastructure, quality controls and financial stability of a legal plan company. Once the producer and client company decide to offer a legal plan, the producer should give careful thought to the approach required to combine the legal plan sale with the disability or life sale. By focusing on the presentation, the producer can offer the new plan without taking enrollment time away from core products. The explosive growth and need for legal plans, coupled with the demand for these plans from employees, makes this an easy voluntary benefit to recommend.

Robert L. Heston, Jr. is president and chief executive officer of the Legal Access Companies, the leading provider in marketing, administering and operating quality legal plans. Robert assumed responsibility for the Legal Access Companies in 1981 and became a pioneer in the early stages of legal plan development. He has been instrumental in the development of the proprietary network management infrastructure utilized by Legal Access Companies. He has also been responsible for innovation on all levels of law firm network development and for establishing a revolutionary law firm provider model that Legal Access utilizes to exceed customer service and quality assurance at all service levels in its legal plans.

Robert is an attorney licensed to practice law in Texas and California and has over two decades of experience in law firm management and client representation. He has been admitted to the Supreme Courts of the States of Texas and California and to the United States District Court for the Southern District of Texas and the Central District of California. He has served on various law practice committees of the American Bar Association and is currently serving on the Board of Mass Marketing Insurance Institute [MI2]. Throughout his career, Robert has been a speaker to both attorney and insurance producer audiences advocating the benefits of quality in legal plans. In addition, he has authored numerous articles for insurance producers on the connection between life and disability insurance sales and legal plans. His expertise has been instrumental in building Legal Access Companies into one of the largest and leading legal plans in the world. Robert resides and works in Houston, Texas with his wife Lisa and two children Bobby and Jackie.

Robert L. Heston, Jr.
President and CEO
Legal Access Plans, L.L.C.
2401 Fountainview
Suite 300
Houston, TX 77057
Phone: 713-785-7400
Email: bheston@legalaccessplans.com
Website: www.legalaccessplans.com

CHAPTER THIRTEEN

Discount Medical & Lifestyle Benefits
. . . low-cost, high-value products that work

TERRY TULLO
PRESIDENT
NEW BENEFITS, LTD

The new age of consumerism is creating an environment in which employees are asked to shoulder more of the financial burden and decisions affecting their health care. The entitlement mentality of the '80s, '90s and early 2000s is no longer economically practical in today's workplace. This poses some daunting dilemmas for employees and employers alike. Employees are looking for affordable health care solutions while employers are searching for innovative ways to attract and retain employees while remaining within their budget.

A March 2007 Towers Perrin survey revealed that the majority of 2,400 employee respondents said their "benefit programs were not very effective at meeting their needs for affordable health care." While most employees agreed they "were primarily responsible for financing and managing their benefits . . . they did not feel their employers were adequately helping them shoulder this responsibility. And their resulting frustration with recent changes in benefits is generating other negative feelings about their company and its leadership, with potentially adverse consequences for productivity and performance."

In the book, *Consumer Driven Health Care: How a Health Savings Account May Save Your Job and Solve America's Two Trillion Dollar Crisis**, author Alan Ayers writes: the United States is transitioning from a health care delivery model that pushes consumers through a maze of confusing systems dictated by employers, government and insurance bureaucracies, to a free and open marketplace based on consumer choice.

"We all agree that health care in a developed country is one of life's necessities—no different than food, clothing, transportation, and housing," Ayers writes. "However, if you look at these other necessities you'll find very efficient supply chains, marked by innovation, delivering products consumers want, when and where they want them, at prices and financing terms they can afford."

For example, the result of a free and open market for food in the United States is the safest and most reliable food distribution system in the world. Consumer choices run the gamut from preparing bulk foods at home to dining in upscale restaurants, with government and charity assistance as a stop-gap in extreme cases. Competition for consumer food dollars spurs constant innovation in product and packaging and with billions spent on marketing, there is never any shortage or rationing of food in the United States. Indeed, Americans spend a smaller percentage of their income on food than in any other developed nation.

By contrast, Americans spend 2-3 times more on medical care than people in other developed countries—traditionally a cost borne by employers. Double-digit rises in the cost of employee benefits have motivated many employers to switch to health plans with higher deductibles, co-pays, and co-insurance. While employers of all sizes and in all industries are struggling, the greatest impact is for small- and mid-sized employers facing tough decisions to retain, add, or lay off staff depending on benefits costs. Small- to mid-sized employers, particularly in service industries, are the fastest growing segment of the U.S. economy and the largest creators of new jobs.

While employers desperately need to reduce (or at least stabilize) employee health care costs, to continually improve margins they also need for their employees to be more productive. Wellness and prevention programs that help employees get and stay healthy and reduce the risk of expensive debilitating illnesses are becoming an increasingly important part of employee benefits programs. Because these programs benefit both employer and employee, employers expect employees to share in the costs of these programs.

Discount cards serve both employers and employees in the new health care marketplace by making a greater range of health care options more affordable for consumers while promoting wellness and prevention.

The Cost of Healthcare

Recently, Towers Perrin released its annual Health Care Cost Survey, which revealed some staggering results enumerating the differences between companies that effectively manage their benefit dollars with good employee satisfaction and those that don't. The findings were based on 170 of the nation's largest employers, totaling 3.5 million U.S. employees. The companies were ranked and placed into one of three categories: high-cost employers that spent the most money on health care dollars, and mid-cost and low- cost organizations that spent the least amount of money on health care benefits.

When comparing two companies (each comprised of 10,000 employees) at opposite ends of the spectrum, the high-cost company paid $30 million more each year than the low-cost company. If you're wondering how this can be, here are some of the traits of organizations whose employees typically paid less: They take a more holistic approach, creating a culture of health where employers and employees take responsibility for health management. They define "consumerism" in broad terms that extend far beyond benefit-plan design. They have a clear focus, identify problems early, explore opportunities and prepare extensive solutions. They have created objectives and measurable targets because they know what doesn't get measured doesn't get managed. They spend a great deal of time on education, awareness and communication. And, because employees are accountable for health care consumption, they offer tools and resources to help.

A holistic approach makes it possible to craft a meaningful benefit plan that reduces employer costs, saves employees money and adds value. As discount medical and lifestyle products continue to gain traction and become an integral part of many benefit portfolios, they also present a viable and cost-effective solution for companies willing to evolve and more creatively deliver benefits to their workforce. Solutions now exist to encompass all aspects of an employee's life while boosting productivity and morale.

Solutions for Savings

Forward-thinking employers know medical discount cards with a core package of non-insurance pharmacy, dental and vision benefits can accumulate savings in no time, especially because one card can be used by an entire family. For example, even if an employee already has a co-pay prescription drug benefit, drugs for critical illnesses and lifestyle conditions may not be included in the formulary. What's more, some insured drug plans have a co-pay for generic medications starting as high as $20.00 per prescription. Often, the discount price for a generic drug may cost less than the co-pay. Additionally, when considering caps on insured dental plans and limited coverage on insured vision plans, discount dental and vision plans can play an important role. They help save on services and hard goods like frames and lenses once the insurance has been exhausted. In many instances, a discount dental and vision plan can reap greater annual savings than some lackluster insurance plans.

Discount Medical Savings Example

Based on national retail price averages, the table below illustrates how a typical family of four can save more than $1,000 each year just by using the chiropractic, pharmacy, dental and vision discount medical programs.

Benefit	**Retail Price**	**Discount Price**	**Savings**
Chiropractor *(Initial visit with 10 follow-up visits)*	$660.00	$210.00	$450.00
Local Pharmacy *(Antibiotic – Zithromax – Z pack 1 g., 4 purchases)*	$247.96	$111.48	$136.48
Mail-Order Pharmacy *(Asthma medication, 1- year supply, Azmacort, 100 mcg)*	$829.08	$715.92	$113.16
Dental *(8 cleanings, 1 filling, 1 crown)*	$1,410.00	$1,121.00	$289.00
Vision *(1 exam, 1 pair of frames)*	$279.95	$191.47	$88.48
Vision *(Contact Lenses – 1-year supply, single vision disposable)*	$192.00	$120.00	$72.00
Annual Family Savings			**$1,149.12**

How Discount Plans Work

Discount medical and lifestyle benefits are elegant in their simplicity and unlike insurance, there are no forms to complete (with the exception of a patient profile for mail-order pharmacy and Phone-A-Doc), no claims to file and no pre-existing condition exclusions. Virtually anyone can take advantage of the savings offered by using a discount card. Members take their card to a participating provider and pay the discounted price at the point of service. Although any organization may choose to privately label its card program, it is the network or vendor name on the back of the membership card that triggers the discount.

Participating Providers

Today, discount cards offer a wide selection of products and services. Participants receive discounts when they go to a participating provider as is the case with benefits such as Pharmacy, Vision, Dental, Physician, Hospital, Chiropractic, and Legal services. Members can locate a provider by calling a toll free number listed on the back of their benefits card and speaking to a customer service representative or by using a search link over the Internet. With benefits such as Phone-A-Doc, Counseling, Nurse Hotline and Identity Theft Prevention, the member contacts the service provider directly by phone or Internet. Quality programs offer a comprehensive list of participating providers (including chains and independents) nationwide. Employers and card purchasers should take this into consideration when selecting a discount medical plan organization to ensure their employees will have adequate coverage in their area.

Discount Benefits

The following is a list of discount medical and lifestyle benefits available to virtually any employer group or individual:

Health Benefits

Alternative Medicine
Chiropractic
Counseling
Diabetic Supplies
Dental Care
Doctors Online
Family Consultation
Hearing Aids
Medical Supplies
Nurse Hotline
Personal Wellness Online
Pet Savings
Pharmacy
Phone-A-Doc
Physician Visit / Hospital
Medical Travel Assist

Long Term/Elder Care
Medical Health Advisor
Medical Records Storage
Vision Care
Vitamins

Lifestyle Benefits

Auto Pricing & Maintenance
Condo Savings
Dining Discounts
Financial Help Line
Fitness Advantage
Flowers For All Occasions
Funeral Protection Plan
Golf Savings
Hotel Savings
Home Security Systems
Home Repair
Identity Theft Protection
Identity Theft Prevention
Interstate Moving
Legal Services
Magazine Service
Movie Tickets
Real Estate
Recreation Discounts
Roadside Assist
Quicken Home Loans
Shopping Service
Ski Savings
Tax Help Line
Theme Parks
Travel Reservations

Discount Cards Keep Employees at Work

The workplace landscape is shifting and employers are evaluating the ever-changing needs of their employees. HR managers need tools and resources to increase productivity, morale and attendance. Offering assistance with balancing work and life pressures is a central factor. While millions of consumers already use discount cards to reduce out-of-pocket costs for health care expenses, now the trend is to include products and services people use every day, like financial help lines, discounts on legal services, auto maintenance and so much more. Offering lifestyle benefits allows employees to save money in all areas of their lives.

Supplemental benefits are typically a voluntary purchase. But because discount benefits are so inexpensive, many employers have discovered it makes sense to pay for certain benefits that address their unique workplace concerns. To keep employees healthy and at work, benefits such as Phone-A-Doc—which allows employees to speak with a doctor and often receive a diagnosis and prescription right over the phone--have proven to save time while addressing ailments before other employees are exposed and possibly infected. Roadside assistance and legal services also help to decrease absenteeism. Among its many features roadside assistance includes towing service, flat tire repair and help with dead batteries. This is a "no excuses" program which virtually eliminates calls from employees saying their car won't start and they can't come in to work.

Discount legal services have become a mainstream benefit. Employees can obtain affordable, capped hourly rates in addition to the preparation of a simple will, review of documents and many other services at no cost. Companies offering this benefit find that employees are less likely to take time off from work to tend to pressing legal matters. But one size does not fit all. The flexibility to customize benefit packages is germane to a holistic solution. Because consumerism is forcing employees to take control, become better educated and assume responsibility for a portion of their health care expenses, offering a menu of benefits allows employees the freedom to select the options that best fit their family's needs and budget.

There should be no confusion about the role discount benefits play in a consumer driven market. They are not an alternative to health insurance, but one part of the solution to lower healthcare costs. The discount industry continues to grow and be vibrant as it has evolved from a cottage industry to a viable and essential piece of the healthcare puzzle. When program participants know exactly what they will pay for their prescription drugs or a pair of eyeglasses for example, it is transparency at its finest. The consumer knows what is owed at the point of service, versus waiting for the claim to be filed and processed to see what portion is still left to be paid. Today the consumer is being asked to make buying decisions based on what they need, not what they want. Unlike insurance where premiums increase with additional dependents and over utilization, discount programs thrive on and encourage consumption. Discount cards are low cost with high value and can easily pay for themselves with just one prescription, eyeglass purchase or visit to the dentist. When you consider only one in ten people ever meets their health insurance deductible, discount benefits are a perfect fit for the other nine.

**Consumer Driven Health Care: How a Health Savings Account May Save Your Job and Solve America's Two Trillion Dollar Crisis*, Roger Blackwell, Thomas Williams and Alan Ayers, Atlas Books Distributor, 2005.

After 18 years with Xerox and Apple, and two years as executive director of a 35,000-member non-profit association, **Terry Tullo** joined New Benefits in 1995 and was promoted to president in February of 2000. New Benefits is a privately held company with more than 100 employees that wholesales and services customized discount health and insurance benefit programs.

As president, Terry takes a hands-on approach to managing the operation and, in order to maintain its distinguished culture, is actively engaged in the hiring and development of New Benefits' employees. As consumer-driven health care continues to evolve, she promotes the concept and the role discount medical programs play through various speaking engagements and published articles. After New Benefits' April 2007 acquisition of miQuotes.com, an Internet insurance quoting and enrollment company, Terry's global focus is to identify and build relationships with organizations that require a fully integrated single-source platform for discount and insurance benefits. She is passionate about delivering flexibility and responsiveness and is well known for creating and implementing the acclaimed quarterly "Dare to Dazzle" program that teaches the practical and philosophical aspects of how to "Wow!" clients and members.

Terry Tullo
President
New Benefits, Ltd
14240 Proton Road
Dallas, TX 75244
Phone: 800-800-8304 x1617
Fax: 972-201-0887
Email: ttullo@newbenefits.com
Website: www.newbenefits.com

Chapter Fourteen

Rounding Out the Benefits

FRANK J. DALLAGO III
Director of Shared Services
Trion

In today's constantly changing labor force, savvy human resources managers know that in order to recruit and retain a skilled and experienced workforce, an employer's compensation package needs to be comprehensive. Employees are seeking flexibility, more benefit options and more control of their work life. Many of today's most progressive companies give employees a full menu of choices, including multiple core benefit options as well as a full range of voluntary benefits and flexible spending accounts. In addition to benefits, flexible work schedules, additional time off and the option to work from home are becoming increasingly common. This gives employees the ability to create work schedules and a benefit package that best fits their lifestyles. In return, employers hope to attract more productive and motivated employees who are committed to long-term employment.

Flexible spending accounts, (FSAs) which have demonstrated increased levels of participation and election each year, represent one part of that comprehensive package. This is a benefit that allows employees to create their own benefit options. Employees use a FSA to fill in the gaps left by traditional health insurance, such as co-pays and deductibles, and find it to be a convenient way to pay for those eligible everyday items. In addition to convenience, FSAs provide significant tax savings. When employees purchase benefits on a pre-tax basis through a FSA plan, their taxable compensation is reduced. This in turn reduces their wages that are subject to federal, Social Security and Medicare taxes and, in most states, state income tax as well. Money that would have been spent after tax is now spent in a FSA plan, saving employees hundreds of dollars each year.

Many companies are still unaware of the advantages to both the employer and employee of offering a flexible benefit program, while others have misconceptions about this benefit. It is shocking to see that smaller employers are still not implementing these plans. Unless an employer has a high degree of turnover, there's really no reason not to offer a FSA. Every employee can use one, and every employer and employee can benefit from one.

Thomas R. Warburton, benefits administrator for Weichert Realtors in Morris Plains, New Jersey, observes:

"Weichert Realtors has always strived to maintain a competitive benefits package that will aid in employee retention as well as making us the employer of choice in the marketplace. We also take into account the impact that offering an affordable, quality benefit lineup has on our employees' professional and personal lives. It is important for us that our employees are happy with the plans that we offer and receive quality coverage."

"For this reason, we began offering a flexible spending account as part of our benefits package. As with most companies, our employees are sharing in the monthly premium cost as well as paying coinsurance amounts, deductibles and any balances that may be left for out-of-network charges. We wanted to offer every opportunity for employees to maximize the money they are spending for health care. With a FSA in place, our employees benefit from the opportunity to put money aside for these expenses while receiving the pre-tax benefit allowed with these types of plans. We have had great success with the flexible spending plan."

What Are Flexible Spending Accounts?

Flexible spending accounts are Internal Revenue Service-approved plans that allow employees to be reimbursed for medical and dependent-care expenses on a pre-tax basis. Pre-tax payroll dollars (including state taxes in most cases) are set aside to be used for eligible expenses.

There are two separate reimbursement accounts within a flexible spending account:

In a health care reimbursement account (HCRA) employees can use pre-tax dollars to pay for eligible medical, dental and vision expenses that cannot be reimbursed through insurance or any other arrangement.

The HCRA can reimburse the employee for eligible expenses incurred by the employee, the employee's spouse and his or her dependents.

Health care reimbursement accounts cover a large list of items and services for which an employee can seek reimbursement. Some examples include insurance deductibles and co-pays, prescriptions and eligible over-the-counter drugs, dental and orthodontia services including braces, durable medical equipment, psychiatric services, vision exams and eye care, including laser surgery. For a comprehensive list of eligible health care expenses, review IRS Publication 502 and Revenue Ruling 2003-102, *Medical and Dental Expenses.*

With a dependent care reimbursement account (DCRA), employees can use pre-tax dollars, up to $5,000 per year, to pay for eligible child and/or adult dependent care expenses that are incurred to allow that employee or his or her spouse to work, look for work, or go to school full time. Eligible expenses include those that qualify for the IRS dependent-care tax credit, such as babysitting provided by someone other than a dependent, day care, day camps, nursery school, or other outside dependent or child-care services and elder care for dependents who live with the participant. For more information about eligible dependent care expenses, review IRS Publication 502, *Dependent care expenses.*

Easy Set-Up

A FSA is established through a Section 125 plan with the creation of a plan document that permits employee contributions on a pre-tax basis. The plan document does not have to be submitted to or registered with any government agency. It is simply an internal company document to support the plan. Typically, employers hire an administrator or a legal or accounting professional to create the plan. The HR department's responsibility for the ongoing administration is minimal when employers have a qualified administrator in place. The administrator provides employees with customer service and performs all data processing. Good administrators also provide debit card access.

The actual FSA enrollment can be done in many ways. A good third-party administrator (TPA) will be flexible enough to accept enrollment information in different ways. Many employers have their own internal enrollment processes set up, which work equally well. The TPA can accept the data from their system, offer online enrollment services or accept paper enrollment forms, which the administrator manually loads.

Health Care FSA Details

For a health care reimbursement account, employers set the maximum employee contribution. Employees select the amount to be withheld from each paycheck based on their estimated annual out-of-pocket health care expense. Typically, employers will limit health care reimbursement accounts to between $3,000 and $4,000 because of the risk factor involved. Because the entire annual election is available to the employee immediately, an employer is at risk if an employee uses the total amount and then leaves the company. However, it is important to note that the average forfeiture amount for a plan is around one half of one percentage point. Most companies that install a FSA plan generally do so to provide their employees with additional benefits, so they are willing to absorb a potential loss. However, very few companies finish a plan year in the negative.

IRS guidelines for tax-deferred plans state that employees must either use the funds or lose the funds. This is commonly referred to as the "use it or lose it" rule. At the end of a plan year, any funds that remain in an employee's account revert to the employer, which can use those funds to offset administrative costs. If the forfeitures exceed the administrative costs, the employer has the option to set those funds aside for future administrative costs or to contribute them back into the FSA plan.

Unless a qualifying event takes place, an employee cannot change a contribution amount or opt out of the plan during the year. Some general qualifying events are a change in marital status, a change in the number of dependents, which means a birth or a death, or a change in employment status. A change in salary is not considered a qualifying event.

Debit Card Details

Debit cards were authorized by the IRS for use with flexible spending accounts in 2003. When a debit card is used, there is no payment at the point of service. When an employee goes to the pharmacy to pick up a prescription, or receives services at a doctor's office, the debit card is used as the form of payment. It eliminates the need for cash and the tedious task of gathering receipts, filling out claim forms and submitting them to the administrator. There is no waiting for reimbursement. The entire process is streamlined.

An Employee Transaction

Consider an employee named Ralph who has a doctor's visit. His health insurance plan includes a $25 co-pay. Ralph hands the receptionist his FSA debit card. The debit card is swiped for the co-pay. Ralph leaves the doctor's office and drives to the pharmacy to pick up his prescription. At the pharmacy he picks up cough medicine and a candy bar along with his prescription. All three items are rung up at the same time on the register. Once again, Ralph hands the clerk his FSA debit card. The debit card is swiped and only the FSA-eligible items, the prescription and cough medicine, are approved. The clerk sees this and asks Ralph for another form of payment for the candy bar. At that point, all of the appropriate FSA information is electronically transmitted to the plan administrator and Ralph's account is immediately updated to reflect the transaction. His eligible or available balance is reduced. When Ralph gets home, he logs on to his account and immediately sees the entire transaction.

One week later, Ralph has to increase his prescription dosage, so he drives back to the pharmacy for an updated prescription. But this time, he forgets his debit card. So he pays in cash, saves his receipt and submits it via mail along with a claim form. Ralph receives his reimbursement in about five days. From this example, it's easy to see how employees appreciate the value of a comprehensive benefits package that gives them flexibility and convenience.

Dependent Daycare Details

Unlike the health care reimbursement account, the dependent daycare account has a maximum contribution of $5,000. It is also available as a deduction from the participant's pay but is not pre-funded, meaning the employee can only spend what has actually been deducted. If married, both spouses must either work, be seeking employment or be full-time students. Both spouses may participate with different employers as long as their total contribution does not exceed $5,000. When one spouse is not actively employed or seeking employment, he or she can no longer participate.

An eligible dependent is one who lives with the participant and receives more than half of his or her support from the participant. It is important to note that a dependent daycare account is not just for dependent children. It is for anyone who requires care, such as a spouse, parent, sibling or anybody else who needs support. The account does not reimburse for costs associated with parents in a nursing home, because the parents no longer live in the participant's home. However, if an elderly parent is being cared for in the participant's home and a neighbor comes by to provide assistance, this qualifies for reimbursement from a dependent daycare account.

The caretaker does not have to be licensed or certified in any way. The caretaker can even be a relative, so long as the caretaker is not a dependent. For example, if a participant's 16-year-old daughter is caring for her 10-year-old brother, the situation is not eligible for reimbursement.

It is interesting to note that for every 1,000 employees who participate in a flexible spending account, approximately 95 percent participate in the health care reimbursement account, 4 percent participate in both the health care reimbursement and dependent care account, and only 1 percent participate in the dependent care account. The reason that the dependent care account has a significantly lower utilization is that for now, the dependent care tax credit is usually more beneficial for people in lower tax brackets than the savings realized with the dependent daycare account.

Access, Employer Misconceptions and Answers

Although access to flexible spending accounts is rapidly increasing, there are wide variations in access based on company size and the characteristics of the employee group. Forty-three percent of white-collar workers have access to FSAs versus 23 percent of blue-collar employees. Forty-five percent of workers with wages above $15 per hour have access, while only 21 percent of workers with wages below $15 per hour have access. While some of this variation may be explained by factors including employee eligibility and the transient nature of workers in some industries, the majority is explained by a more fundamental reason. Many employers are still not aware of the advantages to both the employer and employee of a flexible benefit account. Others have certain common misconceptions:

Objection #1

"We simply can't afford more benefit costs." With benefit costs soaring, some companies feel their benefits dollars are already stretched.

Answer

FSA plans can actually save employers money. Because FSA deductions are made on a pre-tax basis, employers save on FICA and FUTA taxes and, in most states, disability and worker's compensation insurance premiums as well. These savings can be as high as 10 percent of FSA elections and typically exceed the costs of administration.

Objection #2

"It's not worth the administrative hassle." This objection is common among employers that have had a bad administrative experience with a FSA administrator.

Answer

The FSA administration industry is very fragmented and includes many small undercapitalized companies that may provide less than adequate service. However, there are also very good full-service FSA administrators that provide a high level of service, which makes the FSA plan experience simple and convenient. It is important to choose the right administrator; one with a proven track record and all the tools needed to provide great service.

A good administrator will provide support in all phases of administration, including employee communications, enrollment and enrollment processing, claims adjudication, debit card processing, customer service, reporting and compliance support. A FSA administrator should keep current with the latest cafeteria plan regulations and court cases to ensure that a program is administered in accordance with the current regulations, especially as they relate to debit card processing. Core FSA services should be designed to eliminate the administrative burden associated with FSA plan sponsorship. FSA compliance services should be designed to help an employer meet reporting, disclosure and non-discrimination requirements. Web-based technologies should be deployed to deliver the valuable benefits of increased administrative efficiency and around-the-clock access to account information for the employer and employees. In many ways, administrative success depends on how little involvement the employer has in the administrative process.

Objection #3

"We already provide comprehensive benefits and see no value in offering a FSA."

Answer
No matter what medical, dental or vision plans a company offers, there will always be additional out-of-pocket expenses that employees must bear. It makes sense to provide them with a convenient method to handle those expenses while saving them money.

Additional Advantages

Employers that offer flexible spending accounts receive other direct advantages. Since the typical savings achieved at the employer level can represent as much as 10 percent of total FSA contributions, many employers use the savings to pay for the administrative costs associated with these plans. The savings from a FSA can also offset the cost of another benefit or can be used to further enhance the employer's benefit offering. In recent years, many employers have taken additional steps to utilize the full value of a FSA plan and are contributing funds to the FSA in addition to employee-contributed funds. Typically these employer contributions are tied to certain activities that benefit both the employer and employee, such as rewards for preventive care and screening, as well as employee participation in wellness programs. For example, at one company, employees receive $150 in their FSA for completing certain wellness programs such as smoking cessation, weight-loss and stress-management courses. Progressive employers know that healthier, happier employees are better, more productive employees. Finding and retaining the right employees is important to the success of any business. Having a well-rounded employee benefits program is a key to reaching that goal.

Savvy human resources and benefits managers know that flexible spending accounts are an important and valuable addition to any company's benefit package and are simple to implement, easy to administer, and can create financial savings for the company. They know that employees view FSAs as an important part of their benefit package. In today's highly competitive employee market, every advantage is needed to attract the right candidates. Flexible spending accounts are a cost-effective offering that helps to recruit and retain quality employees, while rounding out a comprehensive compensation and benefits package.

The satisfaction of Trion's FSA and COBRA clients is the focus of **Frank Dallago**'s role as director of shared services. He is responsible for enhancing the operations that serve these clients by implementing new systems and processes and effectively deploying staff. Before joining Trion in 2007, Frank spent more than four years enhancing the operations at AmeriFlex, LLC, as its chief operations officer. There, he successfully managed FSA and COBRA operations through the development of procedures, processes and systems.

Frank J. Dallago III
Director of Shared Services
Trion
2300 Renaissance Blvd.
King of Prussia, PA 19406
Phone: 610-945-1050
Fax: 610-945-1050
Email: fdallago@trion.com
Website: www.trion.com

Chapter Fifteen

Total Benefits

TJ GIBB
Senior Vice President, Marketing
KMG America Corporation

In the not-so-distant past, conversations about worksite voluntary benefits occurred outside the realm of traditional group medical, dental, vision, term life and disability coverage and the like. Benefit communication and administration solutions were likely an entirely different conversation.

Today, many forward-thinking benefit advisors are having discussions with their employer clients about all of their employee benefit needs, or their "total benefits." Total benefits refers to the complete package of employee benefits and corresponding services offered by employers.

A Look Back

In order to understand where the employee benefits industry is headed, let's review some highlights of the past.

In the 1980s, employers often purchased all of their benefits from one insurance carrier. Many carriers offered both medical and dental plans, along with ancillary products such as group term life and disability. As we entered the 1990s, managed care began to dominate the health care landscape and many carriers decided to leave the medical insurance business, often opting to focus on group products such as dental, term life and disability instead.

During the 1980s and 1990s, worksite voluntary benefits and group benefits were typically marketed by different carriers and through different types of benefit brokers. The irony is that both distribution channels were marketing to the same employers. As the 90s came to a close, we started to see a few carriers begin to cross-sell both group and voluntary benefits through the group benefits brokers.

Fast forward to 2008. Today, group benefits brokers are the fastest growing distribution segment in the voluntary benefits industry. "Group life and health brokers now control almost 50 percent of the voluntary benefit sales. In 2006, that amounted to over $2 billion in sales and we expect that number to increase more and more over time," says Bonnie Brazzell, of Eastbridge Consulting Group. "Our research shows that over 90 percent of benefits brokers sell at least some voluntary products. In addition, we are starting to see progressive medical plan carriers develop and/or purchase voluntary benefit capabilities. This will result in even more voluntary sales by the group benefits brokerage community."

The Total Benefits Approach

Progressive employers want to provide a total benefits solution for their employee population, but they are not necessarily going to pay for it all. An employer must balance the needs of its employee population with the amount it can afford to pay.

Once the employer-paid benefits are determined, there will likely be some gaps in coverage. The next logical question is, "What products are needed to complement the employer-sponsored plans?" This is where voluntary benefits come in. These could be traditional group products such as dental, vision, life insurance or disability, or they could be individually owned voluntary benefits, such as critical illness, accident, disability, level term or whole life.

It is no longer valid to say, "We need to offer a life plan to give employees more choice in their benefit plan." Maybe you do, but look at your total benefits package. After reviewing the entire plan and conducting an insurance protection-gap analysis, several voluntary benefits may be needed.

Several current market dynamics speak to the total benefits approach:

- Employers are competing for talented employees
- Medical costs consume large portions of benefit budgets
- Health care expense management drives cost shifting and an increase in 'consumerism'
- Employers want the simplicity and ease of a blended product platform

- Employees lack the tools and knowledge needed to navigate their benefit decisions
- Employee self-service creates challenges and opportunities
- Brokers and consultants are called upon to solve the aforementioned issues

Employers

Employers and human resources departments have a difficult challenge. They are asked to provide total benefits that are competitive, while still keeping costs to a minimum. Voluntary benefits can play an important role in providing appropriate coverage and controlling costs. However, as the benefits offered become more complex and the number of available benefits increases, employers need help in the form of a streamlined enrollment and communication strategy that supports the concept of total benefits.

Employees

Over the years, there has been much discussion about American workers' lack of protection against unexpected illnesses or injuries. In the past, paternalistic employers assisted in protecting their employee populations. Today, many employers still have the same good intentions, but they are taking a much different approach by encouraging employees to actively manage their benefit choices, a practice called 'consumerism.'

Consumerism does not end with employees taking responsibility for their insurance decisions. It also requires employees to financially participate in their benefits. For example, many employers are implementing medical plans with higher deductibles and out-of-pocket limits. As a result, at the time of a medical service, an employee will be spending his or her own money until the deductible is met.

Voluntary benefits may be needed to help employees manage the potential financial impact of the coverage gap created by a high-deductible health plan. With the complexity and diversity of the available plans, employees often have difficulty determining the type and amount of coverage that's best for their families. Many simply lack the tools needed to evaluate current or added benefit options.

"For many years, employers have offered benefit choices to their employees," says Paul Kraemer, senior vice president of sales for KMG America.

"The difference now is that many employees are not able to fund the gaps in coverage created by their employer-sponsored plans. In order to obtain the appropriate level of protection, employees need to have both employer-sponsored benefits and voluntary benefits. Employees need to become engaged benefit consumers to make sure they are properly covered."

How do voluntary benefits complement employer-sponsored plans?

Consider the following scenario:

- An employee participates in a high-deductible health plan with a total out-of-pocket amount of $3,000
- The employee becomes seriously ill or sustains a major injury with medical expenses exceeding $3,000
- The employee lacks the savings or other means needed to pay $3,000 in medical expenses
- The employee has no voluntary benefits

Voluntary benefits could help in this scenario. Let's assume the employee's illness was a heart attack, a condition covered by most critical illness plans. If the employee had a voluntary critical illness policy, he or she could have received monetary benefits and avoided a difficult financial situation.

Voluntary benefits are meant to complement existing coverage. The ripple effect from consumerism not only forces employees to make their own choices, but also demands that employers make voluntary benefits available to assist employees.

According to Paul Moore, senior vice president of sales for KMG America, "from a holistic perspective, employers need to determine the broad coverage needs of their employee population. Most employees can only afford to spend a small percentage of their income on insurance, so product offerings must make sense. Employees must identify their personal protection needs and understand how to properly utilize those benefits. This is a huge educational challenge. That is why benefit communication companies are in such a good position to fill this void. Human resources departments need to communicate plan changes, educate employees and enroll their population in their benefit plans. The reality is that many HR departments simply do not have the time or resources to devote to this crucial process."

Benefit Communication Companies and Benefit Enrollments

Benefit communication companies and enrollment firms offer solutions that provide value to the employer, HR department, employees, broker and the enrollment process in general.

- **Assisting HR with the core/voluntary benefit enrollment -** Benefit communication firms communicate all benefits, including all group and voluntary benefit plans. This educational process can be offered in addition to or in lieu of current efforts made by the employer or benefit advisor. Benefit communication firms' counselors typically explain how the product choices complement and enhance the current employer-sponsored benefits. The goal is to educate employees about their protection needs and have them elect the appropriate coverage amounts.

- **Value-added services -** Many value-added services comprise a benefit communication service. One example is a benefit statement that displays the actual benefits elected by each employee. The employer and employee portions of each benefit's cost are illustrated, as well as the impact on the employee's paycheck, including tax implications.

- **Technology Tools -** Benefit communication firms use laptop and web-based solutions to accurately capture employees' benefit elections. Technology tools can go far beyond benefit elections, however. More sophisticated systems integrate benefit enrollment and ongoing administration, including payroll and data transfers to multiple carriers.

  Human resources departments can also use technology to move away from handling routine employee transactions. Technology can be used to automate the many employee-level "transactions" that occur in a benefit program. For example, employees can use technology to update beneficiaries, addresses, telephone numbers and emergency contacts, essentially performing their own data cleansing. As a result, the employer receives a completely accurate database of the employee population.

Benefit Advisors

Benefit advisors, also known as brokers and consultants, play a critical role in providing total benefits to their employer clients. They offer valuable advice about cost-effective benefit alternatives that may include redesigned benefit plans, modified employer funding and total benefits, a combination of employer-sponsored and voluntary benefit plans that provide comprehensive solutions and streamlined administration.

Many advisors have answered the total benefits call. The most successful advisors are able to design solutions that use employer-sponsored benefits as a baseline and voluntary benefits to fill in coverage gaps.

All of an advisor's diligent efforts may fall apart without the right insurance carrier. Choosing a carrier that truly understands the various benefit plans—health, ancillary and voluntary—will result in the best customer experience. As medical carriers further develop their ancillary group and voluntary benefit product capability, enhance benefit communication/education efforts and expand administrative services to streamline benefit delivery, we could see employers wanting to purchase benefits from a single carrier again.

The Future is Now

The employee benefits market is embracing the integrated approach of total benefits. Advisors are already handling total benefits for their employer clients and progressive insurance carriers are following suit by enhancing their capabilities in the total benefits arena. Technology already exists that allows employers to access one system for enrollment, communication and administration, with the capability to generate a single bill and provide a single point of entry to manage benefit plans.

The service experience will only improve for employers and employees. Employer-level benefit plan administration can become much simpler once it is consolidated onto a single platform. Then, offering a consumer-friendly suite of benefits becomes very manageable and educational tools can be utilized to their fullest degree.

Everyone Wins

Total benefits speak to the market and merchant merging together. Employers are able to provide comprehensive benefit coverage and communicate a consistent message to employees. HR departments enjoy reduced paperwork, data cleansing, electronic feeds for benefit providers and the convenience of a single integrated administrative and service platform. Employees become educated benefit consumers with access to affordable benefits and gain a clear appreciation for the value of their benefit program. And finally, the benefit advisor has the ability to address benefit cost containment, solve clients' benefit communication challenges, and enhance their role as a trusted advisor.

As the markets push for simplicity and approaches become more consumer-oriented, it is easy to see the value of total benefits.

TJ Gibb is the senior vice president of marketing for KMG America Corporation, a member of the Humana family of companies. KMG America is a progressive insurance carrier that packages group and voluntary benefit solutions. TJ is responsible for product development, corporate communications, branding, advertising, benefit communication, enrollment technology and web site development.

Prior to joining KMG America, TJ worked for ING Employee Benefits, where he was vice president of worksite marketing and association sales.

TJ is active in various insurance industry organizations and serves on the board of directors as treasurer for the Mass Marketing Insurance Institute (MI2).

He earned a Bachelor of Arts degree in business administration with a concentration in financial management at the University of St. Thomas in St. Paul, Minnesota. He currently lives in Eden Prairie, Minnesota, with his wife Holly and two children, Trevor and Marissa.

TJ Gibb
Senior Vice President, Marketing
KMG America Corporation
12600 Whitewater Drive
Minnetonka, MN 55343
Phone: 952-930-4806
Fax: 952-930-4802
Email: tj.gibb@kmgamerica.com
Website: www.humana.com

CHAPTER SIXTEEN

The Importance of Benefit Communication

LOUIS J. PANTALONE
EXECUTIVE VICE PRESIDENT
UNIVERS WORKPLACE BENEFITS

The landscape of employee benefits in the 21st century is changing. With double-digit premium increases becoming a reality, employers are reducing benefit plans and shifting costs, asking employees to share in a greater contribution. It has never been more critical to help employees understand their options and support their decision-making processes.

In an effort to quantify the value of effectively communicating benefits to employees, Univers Workplace Benefits partnered with Strata Research, an independent research firm, in the summer of 2007 to perform a study at the Society for Human Resource Management's 59th Annual Conference in Las Vegas, Nevada. There, we examined employee benefits and enrollment processes offered by employers in a variety of industries. All respondents who were interviewed participate directly in the administration, enrollment, technology or decision-making process for their respective employers.

Our research was designed to uncover ways in which the benefit enrollment process can be made more efficient for both employers and employees. Additionally, the study shed light on how these interactions affect employee satisfaction, retention rates and the hard and soft costs associated with employee enrollment.

Our findings revealed that regardless of the specific benefit options companies offer, employees who are more knowledgeable about their benefits are more likely to provide high job-satisfaction ratings and less likely to leave their respective companies. Therefore, ensuring that employees comprehend the true value of their benefits is critical.

Successful communication techniques ensure that employees are educated about their benefit options, thereby enriching their enrollment experience and benefiting employers and employees alike. This fact, coupled with our finding that the area of greatest concern for human resource professionals is attracting and retaining employees, illustrates that while the types of benefits available to employees is critical, the first hurdle is educating employees about their benefits offering.

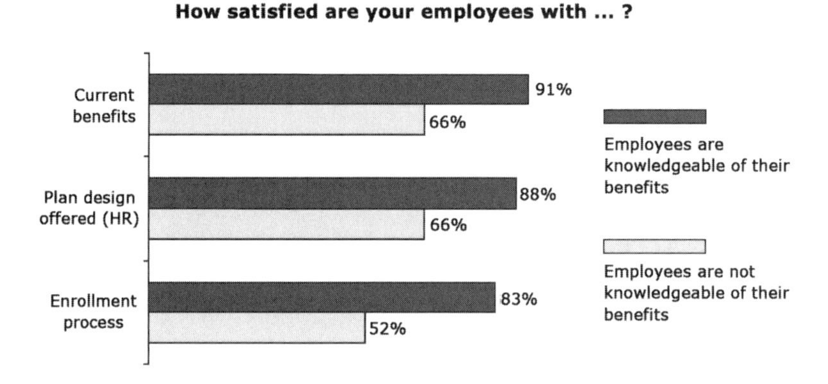

Effective communication can be the most critical element of a benefits plan. A good benefits plan with a poor communication strategy will have poorer employee satisfaction results than an average plan with a good communication strategy.

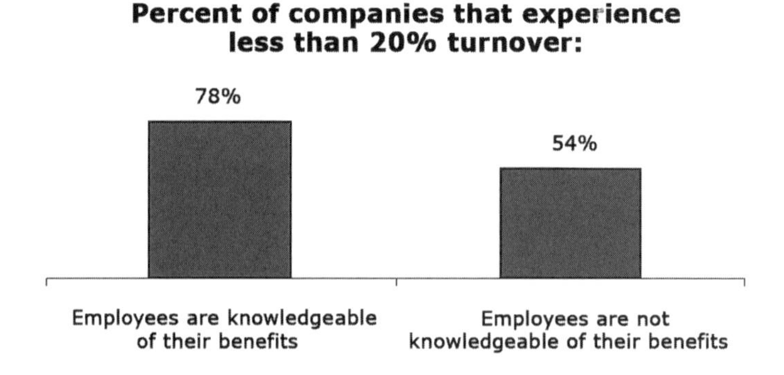

The question then becomes, which methods most effectively educate employees?

Defining Strategies

A large motivation for engaging the services of an enrollment firm is the ability to provide a comprehensive and employee-specific communication strategy.

The choice of pre-communication methods is predicated on the culture of the employer and employee group and the answers to several key questions:

- What methods have been used successfully in the past?
- What does the employee population look like?

In today's market we're dealing with many generations. Baby boomers and younger people work together. People speak different languages. There's a lot of diversity in the workplace. This is important to understand when designing the pre-communication campaign.

Employers are extremely concerned about the amount of time that employees will spend completing the enrollment process. The better we can prepare employees for the enrollment, the more efficiency we can offer the employer.

During open enrollments, employees are often flooded with literature and only read portions of their documents. What they do read may be difficult for them to understand, and their interest in the subject is difficult to engage unless they have a specific and acute need.

One of our company's areas of expertise is in providing pre-communication materials that are simple, easy to read, and that enable employees to work with their significant others, spouses or family members to determine their needs prior to making an enrollment decision.

In our communications, we explain what it costs the employer to provide benefits for the employee. We estimate that 95 percent of employees don't understand how much their employer contributes for their benefits. All they see is what comes out of their paycheck. Our process is designed to show them the contribution that the employer is making on their behalf, illustrating the true value of their paycheck.

Working with the human resources department, we compile the materials needed to create the proper communication vehicles. Once the employer approves the materials, they are distributed at work, mailed to the employees' homes or posted around the worksite or on the Internet.

It's also very helpful to educate the first-line supervisors in group meetings and prepare materials for them to deliver to their staff members.

Enrollment Methodologies

To a large extent, company size dictates the enrollment methods used. Some techniques may be more viable for smaller sized companies, while larger companies require alternative methods to achieve effectiveness.

For example, smaller companies are more likely to utilize face-to-face communication methods such as in-person meetings with employees who have questions about benefit options. This personal approach has proven to be successful in terms of educating staff and increasing benefits awareness.

As the company size grows, however, communication methods become more bureaucratic, with a greater emphasis on efficiency. Companies with more employees gravitate toward benefits fairs and self-service systems. While they do not disregard the advantages of more personal methods of communication, these companies must ensure that their resources are being properly allocated.

The study's most concerning results come from medium-sized companies. Those companies that employ between 1,001 and 5,000 employees are the least successful in communicating with and educating employees about their benefit options.

Companies in this group also had the lowest percentage of employee benefit participation. While a variety of circumstances may contribute to this, one likely cause may be their heavy reliance on paper enrollment aids, which proved to be one of the least successful methods for enrolling and educating employees.

The Preferred Enrollment Methodology

Our study shows that the best enrollment method is face-to-face meetings, which are most often conducted by companies with fewer than 1,000 employees. Our results indicated that smaller-sized companies have employees who are better educated about the benefits available to them, are more likely to take advantage of those benefits, and are more likely to be satisfied with the plan design offered by their employer.

A critical success factor for face-to-face meetings is scheduling, the ease of which depends on the specific workplace environment.

In a manufacturing setting or an assembly line, it is difficult to set appointments. In these situations we employ a "tag system": When one employee is finished with his or her enrollment session, the department supervisor sends another employee. In other environments, like hospitals, individuals can be assigned a specific appointment time.

At times, financial considerations make face-to-face meetings difficult, if not impossible. In some markets, such as retail, there are small groups of eligibility at each location and it's not financially feasible to get to every location. That's when an enrollment call-center method is used. Some types of industries cannot be reached at all and a call center is used exclusively. Outbound call centers do a better job of scheduling people. On the occasions when inbound calls are necessary, we are very clear with the employer that we need to provide a structure for that inbound call.

The Internet also comes into play when employers want to transition to an online self-service module. Many people want to use the web. We survey employees to determine their ability to work online. When employers change their whole methodology and say, "We're going to do it this way this year," without understanding their population, that could cost them a lot of money. They might not obtain the results they want to achieve. Our feedback gives them a good feel for when they can move to that type of enrollment process.

Survey Says?

Because our benefit counselors meet with every employee, we have an opportunity to survey each employee during enrollment. Employers can get their employees' perspective on any corporate initiative, such as:

- Company Communication - "How well do you feel the company communicates new practices, policies and change?"
- Employee Recognition - "How satisfied are you with the recognition you receive for doing a good job?"
- Strategic Benefit Directives - "Would you be interested in "flex dollars" that would allow you to pick and choose which benefits are paid wholly or in part by the company?"
- Understanding Employer Costs - "After speaking with your benefit counselor, do you have a better understanding of how much your employer is contributing to your benefits?"

The compiled results of this survey allow employers to get feedback regarding the effectiveness of the enrollment, the communication of the value of employer-paid benefits, and the quality of counselors.

Billing and Administration

The best executed communication strategies can be cut off at the knees if the benefits an employee elects are not billed or administered correctly.

During the course of the enrollment, the data that is collected from each employee is managed and scrubbed on a daily basis. Within 10 days from the end of enrollment, all of the merged and scrubbed data is transmitted to the appropriate entities, such as the employer, carrier, payroll vendor or third-party administrator, so that billing and contracts can be generated.

Billing is generated by the carriers from the data files that are sent. Providing the employer with the proper deductions to match the original election is critical. Without the proper review and clean-up of the hundreds of thousands of calculations that take place, there can be errors, many because of different rounding rules.

Regardless of how positive the education and enrollment experience is for an employee, if a contract doesn't arrive with benefits that match what the employee elects, or the payroll deduction amount is different from what the employee agreed to during the enrollment, any good will that was fostered will be forgotten and complaints will become the overriding memory of the entire process.

The Final Consideration

While enrollment companies may provide expertise and services with limited out-of-pocket costs for employers, the most effective campaigns are hinged on a strong commitment to the process and partnership from the client. Our process is designed to work when we see all employees and thus, we need to have access to conduct these meetings with every employee. Those employees who do not have the opportunity to meet with our counselors are not prepared for the decisions they are being asked to make, and ultimately can't appreciate the value of these benefits as it relates to a component of their total compensation package.

For a complete copy of our 2007 Employer Benefit Communication Study, please contact us by email at Dani.McCauley@universworkplace.com.

Lou Pantalone is the executive vice president for Univers Workplace Benefits, with a primary focus on integrating a shared-service strategy for Univers' three service centers and carrier relationships. As one of the original co-founders of Custom Benefit Programs, Inc. (now known as Univers Workplace Benefits), Lou was instrumental in the development of Univers' ResourceOne communication and enrollment platform, known as the leading technology platform in the industry. Under his guidance, Univers has received numerous industry awards for quality service and voluntary benefit production. With more than 15 years of experience in the benefit communications and enrollment industry, Lou has managed and coordinated every phase of the enrollment process. He resides in Hammonton, New Jersey, with his wife JoAnn and two daughters, Amy and Ashley.

Louis J. Pantalone
Executive Vice President
Univers Workplace Benefits
897 12th Street
Hammonton, NJ 08037
Phone: 609-561-0240 Ext.4112
Fax: 610-537-9312
Email: Lou.Pantalone@Universworkplace.com
Website: www.universworkplace.com

Chapter Seventeen

Building the "Dream Team"

SUSAN C. BIANCO, CLU
Benefit Enrollment Services, Inc.

The recipe for a successful worksite case does not contain any secret ingredients. In fact, this book provides all the resources you will need to ensure success. However, an effective enrollment team is the key to a positive worksite experience. The individuals who communicate the benefits and counsel the employees are the primary representatives of the agent and the client, as well as the carrier. An employer can give you total support for implementing a voluntary benefits program, but if the enrollment counselors are not knowledgeable, personable, capable and, above all, ethical, it could create major relationship issues on all fronts.

For more than 20 years I have specialized in voluntary benefits and have invested considerable time and resources in building my "Dream Team." By sharing my experiences, my goal is to heighten awareness of the value a professional enrollment team provides on all levels, to all parties involved.

Finding the "Right Stuff"

Rome was not built in a day, and neither is a client relationship or a professional enrollment counselor. Identifying someone who is ideal for this role can be a laborious task. After all, your objective is to enhance the relationships created, not diminish them. Finding the right people is crucial because they are an extension and reflection of you. When contemplating the process of adding to or creating an enrollment team, there are several rules you should observe.

Rule Number One: Do not hire someone who is not a good fit for your organization simply because he or she is already licensed to sell financial services products.

The only issue this practice resolves is the licensing process. The knowledge acquired through the insurance licensing exam is beneficial, but most of it is not applicable to practical sales situations. Any competent potential candidate has the aptitude to learn the nuances of insurance. It is more important to find someone who possesses the real-life skills required. The values and goals of the potential enroller should be aligned with yours and those of your clients and their employees.

Compromising your standards by hiring the wrong person in order to meet enrollment requirements is not a sound strategy. However, hiring the right individual is a strategy that promotes satisfaction for your clients and long-term profits for you. My enrollment team is a perfect example of the "right" people. Fortunately, we are halfway through our second decade together, so our clients and agent-partners have also experienced a great deal of continuity. I can attest that the longevity of an enrollment team adds a priceless element to a client relationship. A true "Dream Team" starts with a solid foundation, making it imperative to build upon it with the "right stuff."

Rule Number Two: Determine the qualifications that are most important to you.

Honesty and integrity should be at the top of your list. When counseling employees, the objective is to advise them based on their needs, not the enroller's need or desire to sell a product. This is one reason why my recommended method of enroller compensation is per diem, rather than commission, which is addressed later in this chapter. A strong work ethic typically accompanies honesty and integrity. Enrollers must take pride in their work and always be willing to perform to the best of their abilities. The most outstanding and desirable enrollment counselors believe in the products they sell and their value to an employee. Their commitment to and passion for helping employees are evident. Consequently, their sales and policy persistency rates are higher.

Personality and attitude also play an important part in the selection process. An enroller must be friendly (not flirty), professional (not stuffy), compassionate (not a psychologist), confident (not pompous) and have the ability to relate the benefits of the plan to the rank-and-file employees as well as the company's executives. An enroller's appreciation for the client's soft-dollar investment in sponsoring a voluntary benefits plan encourages an efficient yet thorough enrollment experience for the client and employees. Needless to say, a professional appearance is also mandatory.

A knowledgeable enroller is also an effective communicator. Comprehensive training is essential to accomplish both of these characteristics. Not only must enrollers be fluent in the technical language of how a product works, but they must also understand contractual provisions and how a particular product may or may not benefit each employee. An enroller's ability to discern these differences and communicate them honestly encourages employee trust that ultimately creates a strong loyalty to the products and providers.

Another consideration is flexibility. If an enroller has the ability to travel when necessary, or to work odd hours (yes, the graveyard shift must always be addressed and, incidentally, it usually has the highest participation rate), the enrollment process will be better able to adjust to the client's work schedule.

Rule Number Three: A highly trained enroller is most effective and proficient.

Once the right candidates have been identified, stringent training is in order. Most insurance companies provide training for their products and, if they have electronic-enrollment capabilities, how to enroll using their system. Ideally they have developed an A-to-Z training manual that includes product specifics, case-underwriting guidelines, policy riders and exclusions, specimen contracts, payroll and billing procedures, etc. Once enrollers have mastered the product, they will be prepared to move on to the next level of training: the real art of becoming a professional enrollment counselor.

Practice does not make perfect, but perfect practice does. As in any sales training, role-playing is an important part of the process. The first step is for the trainer to guide an enroller through a mock employee group presentation so he or she knows the products being communicated to potential buyers. Next is the one-on-one employee meeting segment. First the trainer plays the "enroller" and the enroller plays the "employee." Once roles are reversed and practiced numerous times to reach a satisfactory level of competence, the candidate is taken on site during an actual enrollment. Note that enrollers are compensated for the time they invest in training, but it is usually on a lower pay scale than when actually performing on-site duties.

In addition to product knowledge and sales strategies, your methods of tracking the enrollment progress must be included in the training. Even with the prevalence of electronic enrollments, there are still some manual tracking procedures that must be followed to ensure that all employees are accounted for during an enrollment. Although an electronic enrollment reduces the likelihood of errors, enrollers must be well versed in the administrative aspects of an enrollment. If their applications are incomplete or have errors, this will hinder the policy issue. My employees are responsible for reviewing and processing the applications internally and managing the subsequent customer-service functions. They appreciate working with a truly professional enroller. In turn, a professional enroller knows that each administrative staff member is also a critical part of the team. Working in tandem ensures a cohesive and efficient enrollment for the client.

Rule Number Four: Always dot your "i"s and cross your "t"s.

Good business practice requires that a contract exist between the enrollment counselor and the organization hiring him or her. So, before a new enroller is exposed to a client, have him or her sign on the dotted line.

Some of the provisions to be addressed in an enrollment agreement are:

Compensation – I prefer to compensate enrollers on a per-diem basis primarily for the reason stated earlier in this chapter, but other methods include commission, or a combination of per diem and commission. A pay scale based on factors such as experience, ability, sales and policy persistency aids in establishing fair standard practices and serves as an incentive for the enroller. However, per-diem compensation can present a risk if the case does not generate the premium that was initially projected. A per-diem agreement typically states that the enroller will receive compensation based on the time that he or she is physically at the work site, and not on the products sold. The upside is that the higher the employee participation, the higher the profit. Per-diem compensation also alleviates any perceived or real pressure for the employee to participate.

When using commissioned enrollers, there is always the potential for overselling. Dissention and frustration among members of the enrollment team are also possibilities because of the various probable outcomes. For example, if one enroller is responsible for a department in which the supervisor won't allow the employees to take time off or has an aversion to insurance, and another enroller is placed in a department in which the employees value the products and services, a commission arrangement may cause resentment. Regardless of the method of compensation, the hiring company always absorbs travel expenses.

Confidentiality – Understandably, many employers and employees are concerned about the potential mishandling of their personal information. Because of this, enrollers should not discuss their interviews with other company personnel. Any documents that contain private information should be returned to the enrollment supervisor for proper filing or disposal.

Intellectual property – Many contract enrollers work for various enrollment firms and/or insurance carriers. Because I have invested a considerable amount of time and resources over the past two decades in establishing proprietary procedures and systems, my enrollment contract specifically prohibits a contract enroller from using any of my property for enrollments or any other business outside the scope of my company. Real property such as laptop computers and office supplies are also included in this provision. Additionally, and just as importantly, enrollers are expressly prohibited from soliciting any corporations or their employees for any other form of business not included in the scheduled enrollment.

Required licenses and continuing education – Typically, all enrollment counselors must secure and maintain required state insurance licenses and satisfy continuing-education requirements on their own time, and at their own expense. There are many opportunities for enrollers to expand their knowledge by reading trade journal articles and attending insurance company seminars and industry association events. Taking an active role in their professional association not only enhances their commitment to the industry but also increases their visibility in the insurance community, thereby maximizing their marketability. If you intend to create a team to work exclusively for your company, you may consider absorbing the expense of any non-resident licenses required to solicit business on your behalf and providing additional continuing-education opportunities. It is important to equip your team with all the tools necessary to conduct business on your behalf. A real "Dream Team" becomes a permanent part of your organization, serving as ambassadors to your clients and the community.

It's Showtime!

The work site is where the real education takes place. By observing a more experienced colleague, an enroller can become extremely familiar with the sales and application processes and learn first hand the best way to conduct an employee interview. Electronic enrollments and paper enrollments each have unique elements that should have been addressed during the product-information sessions, but having a bird's-eye view of any unexpected glitches is a superior training ground. For example, suppose employees are scheduled to meet with an enrollment counselor in 15-minute intervals, but one is delayed, causing a severe overlap over the course of an hour. During this time, an entire assembly line goes down and the supervisor decides to use the down time to send the whole group in to meet with the enrollment counselor(s). Panic could easily ensue, but skilled enrollment professionals will handle the situation creatively, professionally and, most likely, profitably by capitalizing on the opportunity. This scenario is based on an actual experience. Things do not always go as smoothly as we would wish. Therefore, it is wise to plan for contingencies by practicing different scenarios when holding your training sessions.

After several on-site observations, the enroller will be prepared to meet with employees on a supervised basis. It is imperative that the enrollment supervisor, or another experienced team member, be on site to work directly with the new enroller. Inevitably a question will be asked that would require seasoned knowledge or direct access to the insurance company. The supervisor must use his or her own discretion to determine when to release the enroller to full unsupervised duties. Once this has been accomplished, it's showtime!

Not Just a Win-Win

The concept of worksite marketing is not new. In fact, it was born decades ago but has evolved into one of the most rapidly growing segments of the financial services industry. The products and distribution methods have also evolved, but there has always been one constant: the desire to provide quality products and services to the consumers who are typically ignored by most agents. Worksite marketing does not just create a win-win situation. It is the key to a win-win-win-win situation. Employers are seeking ways to reduce or offset the cost of their fringe benefits; employees are more aware than ever of the need to provide security for their families; insurance carriers are continually striving to increase their market share, profits and visibility; and insurance professionals are pursuing various ways to attract and retain clients while increasing their bottom line. But without a "Dream" enrollment team, none of these goals will be met to anyone's satisfaction. Once the ground work is laid and the team is in place, you can be confident that the needs of your clients are being met, that employees are making informed and responsible decisions for their futures, that your insurance company's production expectations are being met, and that your own company's bottom line is being enhanced.

Susan Bianco began her insurance career in 1982 with a focus in the mass marketing field. In 1988, she founded Benefit Enrollment Services, Inc., a company that specializes in the communication and enrollment of voluntary payroll-deducted employee benefits. Susan has been responsible for the successful enrollments of numerous major corporations headquartered in northern Ohio and has been a featured presenter on the topic of voluntary benefits at many national, state and local forums. She has been published in *Advisor Today* and *Life Insurance Selling* and authored a continuing-education video program that is used by more than 60,000 members of the National Association of Insurance and Financial Advisors.

Susan is a life and qualifying member of the Million Dollar Round Table and has achieved Court of the Table status for many years and Top of the Table in 2002. She is also a member of many other professional organizations including the Mass Marketing Insurance Institute and the National Association of Insurance and Financial Advisors (NAIFA). She served as a board member of the Cleveland Association of Insurance and Financial Advisors from 1993 to 1999 and completed her term as president in 1998, when she was also awarded the prestigious Third Life Award. Susan served as a trustee for NAIFA-Ohio from 1998 to 2000. In 2004, she was re-elected and is currently the organization's vice president.

In 1997, Susan was named one of the Top Ten Women Business Owners of Northeast Ohio by the National Association of Women Business Owners and was featured *by Crain's Cleveland Business* as one of Cleveland's "Women of Influence." In 2002, she was named one of the 500 Most Successful Women in Northeast Ohio by *Northern Ohio Live* magazine.

Susan C. Bianco, CLU
Benefit Enrollment Services, Inc.
8180 Brecksville Road, Suite 110
Cleveland, OH 44141
Phone: 440-838-1320
Fax: 440-838-8750
Email: sbianco@besibenefits.com
Website: www.besibenefits.com

Chapter Eighteen

Enrolling With Style

PATRICIA J. REDIC
President
Succeed With Style

Employees have individual motives for buying our benefits. Some consider their needs and others look at the price, but to some extent, all employees make their buying decisions based on the person enrolling the benefit. They wonder, "Does he have my best interest in mind? Does she know what she's talking about? Do I feel at ease with this person?" And although employees may not consciously recognize this, they are searching for a feeling. "Is the enroller presenting the benefits to me in a way that makes me comfortable to buy?" Employees want to be approached from their perspective, not ours.

I have spent years selling the non-tangible benefit of life insurance and other voluntary benefits to employees in all types of businesses. Throughout any given year, my enrollers and I make thousands of mini sales presentations to every kind of person imaginable. Typically, each employee is allowed only a brief 10 minutes to visit with us one on one. In those few moments, we must become instantly appealing and make a compelling enough presentation that 40 to 90 percent of the employee population feels comfortable enough to sign up for one or more benefits. There's no second chance here. There is no time to develop a relationship. They walk in, they walk out. We must instantly speak their language.

Four Styles

Each of us can quickly establish a good rapport with approximately 25 percent of the people with whom we come in contact. If, during a sales presentation, the person across from me does not like or share my particular style, I may not make the sale. My personal preference is to quickly get to the point. I'd rather skip the preliminary chitchat about golf scores, television shows or the weather. What I would like to say is, "What do you need, here's what I have, let's do it!" Am I thinking from my customer's point of view? Am I delivering information in the way they want to hear it? Twenty-five percent of the time, when my customer shares my personality and behavioral style, the answer is yes. And 75 percent of the time, the answer is no. Selling to just one out of four customers is not good enough.

There are four distinct types of buyers: those who want quick answers and the bottom line, those who want to talk and have a good time, those who want to have a relationship with you and get to know you, and those who want lots of information and accurate details. If you pay attention to their behavior, each will tell you what you need to know in order to sell to them. Armed with that information, you can modify your reactions to adapt to each buyer's preference.

Many people initially say, "I'm not going to change the way I act just to make a sale." Yet you adapt to people and their personality styles every day. You don't relate to your co-workers in the same way that you relate to your children. And you don't interact with your office manager in the same way that you interact with your mother. It's not about changing who you are, but more about understanding what the other person needs and caring enough to accommodate those needs.

A Look Back

Throughout the ages, almost every philosopher has determined four distinctive personality and behavioral types. For Hippocrates it was Sanguine, Choleric, Phlegmatic and Melancholic. Carl Jung identified the Feeler, Thinker, Sensor and Intuitor (the basis for the Myers-Briggs Type Indicator - MBTI®). Keirsey calls them Idealists, Rationals, Guardians and Artisans, and Marston classified Dominant, Influentual, Steady and Conscientious (DISC).

DISC is a four-letter acronym that represents the four behavior dimensions or characteristics of all human behavior. Dr. William Moulton Marston, who was a professor at Columbia University in the 1920s, observed that people behave in different ways and created the DISC perception model as a way to understand and manage those differences. The DISC model provides a common language that people can use to discuss what behaviors they share with others and what they do differently. People with similar styles tend to exhibit specific behavioral characteristics common to that style. All people possess these four styles in varying degrees of intensity. To better understand how to use this information during an enrollment, let's take a look at the most obvious traits of the four personality types:

Dominance: Direct and Decisive

Strong-willed, strong-minded people who take action and demand immediate results.

Influential: Optimistic and Outgoing

"People people" who share ideas, and energize and entertain others.

Steady: Sympathetic and Cooperative

Helpful people who prefer to work behind the scenes, perform in consistent and predictable ways and are good listeners.

Conscientious: Concerned and Correct

Organized people who plan ahead, employ systematic approaches and insist on quality and accuracy.

Pace & Priority

A personality is not one dimensional. In fact, personality is like a ball. It's rounded, resilient and three dimensional. It can change with the circumstances, the mood of the person and the desired outcomes. Similar to a right-hand or left-hand preference, most people have a natural and preferred default personality and behavioral mode. So even though there are many aspects involved in a personality, you can easily begin to recognize a person's style by looking for two things:

Pace: Is the person fast paced or moderately paced?

Priority: Is the person focused on the task at hand or involved with people?

You can identify pace from a person's speed of speech, body movements and general energy level. You can determine priority from the focus of the conversations. Is it about the bottom line and results? Is the person questioning, looking for logical answers and facts? Or does the person seem to be accepting, with talk about emotions, feelings, relationships and people?

Pace and priority are the first two things to discover during your initial introduction to someone else. They are the easiest to determine in a short amount of time. Watch and listen to the employees as they enter the enrollment room. Notice their pace and priority. When you accommodate the other person's style, you'll easily succeed at creating a strong first impression, which smoothes the way into the rest of your presentation.

What to look for and how to respond

Once you've discerned the employee's pace and priority, here are a few ways to appeal to that person and make the sale.

Dominant people want results and control. *What* does the benefit do for them? They typically *tell* you what they want in a strong, direct manner. They decide quickly when results are perceived.

As they enter the enrollment room, you will notice:

Pace: Fast

- Businesslike walk
- Direct eye contact
- Speaks rapidly

Priority: Task

What they might say:

- "So what are you selling?"
- "What's this all about?"
- "Is this going to take long?"

Presentation Preferences:

Limit socializing, get to the point, anticipate 'What' questions, emphasize efficiency and savings, and accept their bluntness. Show your desire to help them achieve added results. Provide options. Allow them to make the decision. Make a direct close.

- Likes fast-paced presentations
- Wants a few result-oriented options
- Brief meetings with accomplishments

What They Want From You:

- A fact-based, bottom-line presentation
- Viable options
- Brief pros and cons
- Key points
- A way to win
- Results

A note from practical experience: This type of style is easy to spot. When a no-nonsense dominant style enters the enrollment room, you must be prepared to quickly and succinctly say, "Here's what we have, here's how it works, which do you want?" This is not a time to fumble with lots of words, long-winded presentations or slow-moving computer screens. These folks will not hang in there with you. The rest of the employees usually trust the opinions of the dominant employees, so it is important to the outcome of the enrollment that they have a positive experience with you.

Influential people want people involvement and recognition. *Who* else buys or uses your benefits and what are others saying about it? They usually *tell* about ideas and accomplishments. They decide suddenly after perceiving that the two of you are on the same wavelength.

As they enter the enrollment room, you will notice:

Pace: Fast

- Large gestures, moves quickly
- Speaks rapidly, frequently and dynamically
- May come in pairs or groups
- Casual and friendly demeanor

Priority: People

What they might say:

- "How many other people have signed up?"
- "Did Gina in accounting take this plan?"
- "Can the three of us come in at the same time?"

Presentation Preferences:

Be casual and friendly. Relate to their feelings and aspirations. Be enthusiastic. Ask open-ended questions to reveal their motivations. Anticipate *who* questions. Emphasize how they will save effort and how your product or service increases their influence with and approval by others. Use testimonials from others. Use an assumed close.

- Likes a presentation with broad overviews and no written details
- Likes the big picture versus specific tasks
- Wants to know the positives

What They Want From You:

- Presentation with lots of enthusiasm and emotion
- No fine print and lots of testimonials
- Atmosphere of people and events
- Feelings
- Positives
- Fun

A note from practical experience: If you have sign-up sheets or appointment schedules prior to the enrollment, and two people sign up for one time slot, they will most likely be of the influential style. Influential employees bring some fun and humor into the enrollment room. Their incessant talking makes them easy to spot. This style appreciates offerings of donuts, cookies or candy to help make the enrollment a party-like event. Like their dominant counterparts, these employees are fast paced and do not savor slow-moving computer software or tiny printed marketing materials. They do best eyeball to eyeball in order to get a feeling of who you are and how they feel about you. This is the time to find common ground and tell them about other similar enrollments. Name names if you can and let them know they are in good company. Re-enrollments and influential personalities are a priceless pair. You can encourage new employees to take part because so and so in their department has been a client for years. Existing influential clients are more than happy to help recruit new employees. Remember, it's all about *who* for these folks.

Steady people want security and stability. *How* will the benefit help stabilize conditions for them? They tend to listen with some expression of acceptance and decide after hearing enough to indicate that you clearly understand their needs and are prepared to meet them.

As they enter the enrollment room, you will notice:

Pace: Moderate

- Shy to enter the room
- Warm and friendly
- Slow and methodical demeanor

Priority: People

What they might say:

- "How does this policy work?"
- "Can I talk to my husband, wife, parents?"
- "Do you want me to send anyone else from my department?"

Presentation Preferences:

Be informal and low pressure but methodical. Be sincere. Focus on questions that demonstrate concern for the relationship. Anticipate *how* questions. Give them the support provided by you or your company. Acknowledge their feelings. You may need to probe for real concerns. Give personal attention and follow up. Seek a firm commitment without pushing.

- Likes a slower, methodical presentation
- Likes to decide slowly
- Wants to maintain the status quo

What They Want From You:

- A welcoming, non-threatening greeting
- An informal, low-pressure, conversational presentation with a sincere focus on their needs
- A guarantee of minimal risk – that they can cancel at any time
- A pat on the arm for reassurance
- Reference to family and friends
- Safe, predictable methods

A note from practical experience: Because this is the least flamboyant of the styles, this personality is the most difficult to assess upon initial introduction. You may need to identify this personality through a process of elimination. This type will be the one who has no intention of purchasing a benefit, but will quietly listen to your presentation in its entirety, thank you politely and leave the room, while you are left wondering why he or she just didn't say no from the start. I used to think that either the person was being rude or that I did something wrong. Now I know that you cannot expect a steady personality to behave like a dominant one. However, once this personality becomes a client and realizes your ongoing support, thanks to quality post-enrollment service, you will have a friend and client for life who will do what they can to help you during the enrollment. Like the influential employee, the steady can be a great ally.

Conscientious people want accuracy and order. *Why* is your benefit a logical investment for them? They listen in a controlled manner, asking key questions. They decide after all of the facts are analyzed and the desired results are no longer in doubt.

As they enter the enrollment room, you will notice:

Pace: Moderate

- Slow, precise walk
- Reserved demeanor
- Copy of payroll stuffer with markings and notes
- Paper and pencil for note taking

Priority: Task

What they might say:

- "How long have you/the carrier been in business?"
- "Do I have to decide today?"
- Tend to use the word "investment"

Presentation Preferences:

Get to business swiftly but tactfully. Don't invade their space. Let them be the expert. Be businesslike. Ask questions that allow them to express their knowledge and apprehensions. Anticipate *why* questions. Emphasize the accuracy, logic and quality of your solution. Give them data to support your product or services track record. Use a direct close after allowing time for consideration.

- Likes presentations that are to the point - no chit chat

- Trusts data, numbers and facts versus your opinion
- Wants all the substantiating information

What They Want From You:

- A presentation that gives lots of information and statistics
- Plenty of time to absorb data
- Technical details
- Consistency
- Accuracy
- Proof that you know what you are talking about

A note from practical experience: Unlike the influential and steady styles, this employee wants your knowledge, not your friendship. And like the dominant personality, the conscientious employee is concerned about the bottom line, yet is not in a hurry to achieve the result until he or she understands everything. There is no need to offer sample policies, spreadsheets or carrier ratings, but have them on the table in case a question should arise. And most importantly, be thoroughly familiar with the policy language, know where to find the answer within the policy and understand every facet of how the policy works. Enrollers should demand this type of information during pre-enrollment training. When an employee walks in with a pad of paper and a pen or a copy of the enrollment announcement letter, they are begging you to notice and understand what they need. You can put their mind at ease and let them know that you recognize their preference by saying, "Hopefully you won't need to write anything down. I have brochures and papers to go over with you that explain and address everything." Even if you ultimately do not have the answer to every question, the employee will appreciate your attempt to accommodate them.

It's All in the Presentation

When you deliver your sales presentations, it is important to present your ideas in the way your prospect wants to receive them. Either include a bit of something that each style wants to hear, or craft a slightly different presentation based on each of the four styles. Here are some more ideas to incorporate into your presentation designs.

Dominant people prefer to tell, and tend to decide quickly based on the facts. Therefore, it is best to ask questions such as:

- "We're offering three benefits today: a life insurance plan, a critical illness plan and an accident plan. Which one would you like to hear about first?"
- "You can select between what $5 per week buys or as much as what $20 per week buys. Which deduction option makes sense for you?"

Note: This approach gets to the point quickly and allows them to feel in control.

Influential people prefer to tell and tend to decide based on relationships, so it is best to ask questions such as:

- "Who would you like to name as beneficiary?"
- "You mentioned your daughter's birthday party next week. Would you like to add your children to the policy?"

Note: This approach keeps their priority of people and relationships in mind.

Steady people prefer to ask questions and tend to decide after hearing enough to feel comfortable that you will take care of them, so it is best to tell rather than ask questions:

- "Here's my card with my personal phone number. Feel free to call me any time you have questions. I make it a point to be available to all of my clients at all times."
- "We've enrolled this store for four years now, so I'll be back again next year to check in with you."

Note: This approach allows them to feel safe and reduces the level of risk they perceive.

Conscientious people prefer to ask and tend to decide after analyzing all of the facts, so once again, it is best to tell rather than ask questions:

- "Here's the process. Deductions will begin next Friday the 12th, but your coverage is effective today. Let me show you the brochure that highlights that fact."
- "The policy will be mailed to your home in three weeks, so you'll have an opportunity to read it through in its entirety."

Note: This approach shows them that you too are no-nonsense and care about the details.

How to Speed-Read a Group

What if you are conducting a group enrollment meeting? How do you adapt your presentation to accommodate many people at the same time?

It's not easy to figure out a group of people in a split second, but you can try to work with the party as a whole.

Start off by giving your basic benefits statement in four ways:

1. D – quickly, with vision and results in mind
2. I - with an emphasis on the people aspect, using testimonials
3. S - with a service spin
4. C - with facts and logical options

Deliberately craft the statement in four ways that say the same thing. That gives you a starting point and covers all of your bases. Once you get some feedback or clues, you can start giving more information in that direction. The goal is to blend your message in such a way that the information is accessible to each style.

Flip Charts with Style

One of my first core benefit enrollments was at a hospital. We hired 15 enrollers and conducted three days of training. As the owner of the case, I enrolled and managed the event. Each day, I made time to visit the various enrollment rooms to listen to the presentations. It was interesting to observe the meshing and clashing of personalities. Between the never-ending stream of employees, enrollers and various presentation methods, I got my first "aha" lesson in style recognition. Even though all of the enrollers had the same pre-enrollment training, it was interesting to watch how some naturally made more connections and more sales than others. I also heard some frightening statements that made me wonder if we might get in trouble in the future.

This experience inspired me to create a flip chart presentation, in an effort to bypass enrollers' ad lib attempts and to standardize the event. Over time, the flip chart evolved into something much more significant. It became a marketing tool. We used it during the closing of a case to allow the employer to feel comfortable that the employees would have a consistent enrollment experience. The flip chart was designed to present the benefits in a way that accommodates the employees' various personality and learning styles, all in one neat package.

What's Inside?

The flip charts reflect the products, carriers, underwriting and rates involved with each particular enrollment. For example, if we are offering life insurance, critical illness and an accident policy, the flip chart contains important pieces taken from the carriers' brochures that highlight each benefit. The first page briefly addresses who we are as a benefit company and why the employer chose to offer the benefits. The next page reveals the carriers' names and makes a quick mention of their ratings and sometimes shows a picture of their logo, building, etc. Next, the flip chart highlights eligibility and underwriting questions. There's no point in wasting everyone's time explaining benefits and tantalizing employees if they cannot qualify for the benefit.

Once the qualification factor is addressed, we highlight the features and benefits of the product offer. All of the pages include elements that appeal to the four personality styles. If a dominant style comes in, there are pages we can avoid in an effort to get to the bottom line. Sometimes, after a few pages of the flip chart, it is apparent that we need to jump right to the rate sheet. Why risk losing an interested buyer by insisting they listen to every word of our presentation? When a conscientious style comes in, we have pages at the back of the flip chart that contain policy language, sample illustrations, examples of claim forms and anything else that might contribute to better understanding, along with the carriers' brochures that reiterate the message of the flip chart. A steady employee enjoys the predictable, methodical presentation that a flip chart offers. And an influential employee appreciates the speed, the colorful graphics and the 'big picture'. We move through the pages and adjust our pace and priority as dictated by the behavior of the employee.

The flip chart, coupled with the ability to read and quickly adapt to each employee's buying preferences makes for easier enrollments and has consistently doubled our enrollment results.

Worksite Enrollment Quiz

Now that you have a basic idea of the four personality styles, here is a collection of common enrollment-day one-liners and their corresponding styles. As you read, think about your past experiences and potential future responses and actions.

1. I already have coverage that my parents bought for me when I was two. I don't think I need any more. Is it okay if I come back tomorrow to decide? *(Steady – dislikes change, slow to make a decision)*
2. I want the cancer plan! *(Dominant – bottom line, get it done, decides quickly)*
3. Do I have to decide today? I want to go home and look at all of my other policies and call my agent to see how this compares. *(Conscientious – needs details, accuracy, decides slowly)*
4. Hi, Mary wants to sit in with me. *(Influential – people involvement, social recognition, will buy if Mary buys or may encourage Mary to buy)*
5. What do I do when I want to increase coverage or change beneficiaries? *(Dominant – asks* what *questions, wants to know the options, wants control and results)*
6. How would I cancel this? *(Steady – needs assurances and guarantees)*
7. Do you have something that shows me the cash value I'll have at age 65, 55, 45, 35 and next week? *(Conscientious – needs data, preferably in writing)*
8. Has anyone else taken this coverage yet? *(Influential – wants to be accepted socially, needs testimonials)*

This type of training, awareness and forethought is not only applicable during an employee presentation or enrollment, but also when you are prospecting and meeting employers and HR staff for the first time. Once you've identified your prospect's personality style, you can shift your own approach, style and message to match it. This adaptive selling approach allows the prospect to feel comfortable enough to respond favorably to your ideas. Keep in mind that in order to communicate for results, it's vital to know your own style first. Once you understand your own preferences, it becomes easier to adapt your natural style to meet the needs of your prospects.

It's an indisputable fact that people like to do business with people they like. Relating to people according to their personality style means you treat them the way they want to be treated. When you make a presentation geared to your prospect's particular style, you'll have a much better chance of gaining their cooperation and ultimately, making the sale.

Get ready for your next enrollment. Build a winning presentation using style!

Pat Redic began her insurance career with New York Life Insurance Company in 1992 and for 13 years, sold life insurance and annuities as a registered representative for NYLIFE Securities, LLC. Early in her career she began to specialize in worksite marketing and was asked to create New York Life's voluntary payroll deduction training video as well as mentor new agents.

As president of Millennium Benefits Group, a national employee benefits company, Pat oversees daily operations while building new companies. She is the co-owner of Star Properties, a real estate investment project in Arizona, and Millennium Star Publishing, LLC. She is also president of Succeed With Style, a coaching firm that helps sales professionals become more successful through an awareness of personality styles. She is qualified to offer the DISC personality profile through Inscape Publishing, and the Myers-Briggs Type Indicator® (MBTI) through Consulting Psychologist Press. Her training courses, "How to Make More Sales in 7 Easy Steps" and "How to Become the Best Enroller on the Planet," incorporate these and other insightful assessments.

Pat is a frequent speaker at insurance and sales events, and has served on two insurance company advisory boards. She has been published multiple times in industry magazines including *Life Insurance Selling, Broker World, Benefits Selling, Senior Market Advisor* and the *NYLIC Review*, as well as other national sales publications. Her newest book, *Succeed with Style – Make More Sales Faster*, is now available through Millennium Star Publishing.

Patricia J. Redic
President
Succeed With Style
46 Chagrin Plaza #103
Chagrin Falls, OH 44022
Phone: 440-286-2010
Fax: 440-286-2084
Email: pat@succeedwithstyle.com
Website: www.succeedwithstyle.com

CHAPTER NINETEEN

It Isn't Sold Until it's Enrolled

CHRISTOPHER BERNARDINE SR., CES
MANAGING DIRECTOR
EMPLOYEE BENEFIT COMMUNICATIONS

In the worksite industry, employers, employees, benefits brokers, carriers and enrollment firms tend to measure the success of a worksite case by the results of the enrollment. The focus is on the number of employees seen and the number of employees who purchase benefits. The enrollment process is considered the cornerstone to the success of the program, as well as the key to ensuring the satisfaction of the employer and employees. However, all of the time and effort spent, plus the cost incurred, is wasted if the enrollment isn't implemented and executed properly. The enrollment must benefit all parties while providing ease of communication, education and enrollment for employees.

The first step to a successful voluntary benefits program involves the implementation and enrollment of these benefits. In this chapter, we will discuss the various enrollment options, implementation strategies and the delivery or presentation.

Every organization has a unique set of requirements and concerns that need to be addressed in the planning of the enrollment process. An implementation meeting is necessary to discuss how to make the benefits available to all employees while minimizing the disruption of essential business activities. Let's review how the implementation process works and then determine the proper method of enrollment.

Once a company decides to offer voluntary benefits to its employees, dates for the enrollment are tentatively set. The benefits broker, sales executive and enrollment firm should participate in an implementation meeting, with all parties involved, to develop the right strategy for success. This meeting will determine the timeline, enrollment dates, carrier, products, awareness campaign and the appropriate form of enrollment.

A good way to create an agenda is to ask the following questions:

- Why does the employer want to offer the program to employees?
- Who will be offered the program?
- What will be offered to employees and what will be discussed?
- When will the meetings take place?
- Where will the meetings be conducted?
- How will the enrollment offerings be presented?

Methods

There are many ways to enroll benefits, however, the most popular are face-to-face enrollments (which include one-on-one meetings, group meetings or a combination of both) and telephonic enrollments (which can be inbound or outbound), core enrollments and Web enrollments. Let's review each method to see who and what drives the decision.

Face to Face

For years, a face-to-face enrollment has been considered the most successful of enrollment methods. Face-to-face enrollments are an efficient and effective way to communicate existing and new benefit offerings to employees.

A face-to-face enrollment is implemented by working closely with the employer, carrier and broker. The process begins with a series of announcement letters that generate awareness of the products or programs. These announcement letters should ideally be sent on behalf of the employer on the company's letterhead, encouraging employees to meet with a benefit specialist to discuss their benefit options. The next step is to schedule employee meetings consisting of group only meetings, group followed by one-on-one meetings, or solely one-on-one meetings, taking into consideration the need to avoid disruption of daily work activities. Individual one-on-one meetings offer the greatest satisfaction level for employees and the highest rate of participation. An alternative is the combination of group and one-on-one meetings. According to an Eastbridge study on enrollment practices, 64 percent of small benefits brokers say they typically use a combination of group and one-on-one meetings for their enrollments.

One-on-One

Once a one-on-one enrollment has been determined to be the most effective for the employer and the employees, the implementation of the program begins. There are many factors that must be considered when determining the number of enrollers or benefits specialists needed. Consideration must be given to the specific aspects of each case, including the length of the enrollment period, the number of employees to be seen, and how many employees the employer can afford to have in meetings at one time without impacting productivity.

Locations for the one-on-one meetings must also be determined. Careful consideration must be given to the location of the meetings in an effort to minimize the amount of time an employee is away from his or her job. It is not uncommon for an enroller to relocate at various times throughout the enrollment in order to accommodate each department of the company. The enrollers should be located in private or semi-private areas with a desk or table, chairs and a power outlet for a laptop computer.

On average, an enroller can see 12 to 20 employees per day, depending on the content of information being communicated, as well as the number of products being offered. The average meeting with an employee lasts between 10 and 30 minutes.

Once the number of enrollers or benefit specialists is determined, the next step is to schedule a managers' or supervisors' meeting. This meeting should take place prior to the enrollment and can make the difference between a good enrollment and a great one. First and foremost, it allows the person coordinating the enrollment to build a solid, cooperative relationship with the managers or supervisors. The meeting gives the management team a chance to preview the products, learn when and where the enrollment will take place, and see an overview of the information that will be presented to their employees. By doing so, they can prepare themselves to answer any preliminary questions that may be asked by their staff. This meeting will also allow you to work with the management team to identify any specific restrictions and/or scheduling conflicts for each department.

Scheduling employees can be done in many ways. Two of the most popular approaches are scheduling times for each employee based on shifts, schedule and workflow, and the "tag team" method. Scheduling a specific date and time for each employee allows employees and supervisors to plan their days accordingly. The "tag team" method begins with the first employee seen, as determined by a supervisor. Once the employee's meeting is finished, he or she returns to work and informs the next employee in the department that the enroller is ready to meet with them.

Group Meetings

Group meetings and group meetings followed by one-on-one meetings are the methods most preferred by benefits brokers. Like one-on-one meetings, they are introduced by announcement letters and posters. Group meetings can be mandatory or voluntary. Mandatory group meetings are preferred by benefits brokers, carriers and enrollment companies and increase participation levels.

Group meetings are designed to provide an overview of the available benefits to all employees. Depending on the size of the employee population and number of locations, multiple group meetings may be held to accommodate all employees. Employees can then enroll during or after the group meeting or in individual one-on-one meetings following the group meeting. The individual one-on-one meetings can be scheduled by a sign up sheet and offer employees an opportunity to receive detailed descriptions of the benefits, ask specific questions, determine cost and/or enroll in their chosen benefits.

Telephonic Enrollment

A telephonic enrollment is an efficient, cost-effective way to contact employees when logistics make them otherwise inaccessible because of travel, work schedules or access. They are also a viable alternative when face-to-face meetings are inefficient in terms of time and resources required. This method provides a means to enroll larger organizations that include multiple locations or a few employees at each location. It can also be used in conjunction with face-to-face meetings for employees in remote locations, unavailable employees or those who need additional time to decide on their benefits. It is also an effective way to enroll new employees as they become eligible for benefits.

When selecting a call center to help with a telephonic enrollment, look for a center that has voice-recording and voice-stamping of applications. This eliminates the need to send the applications to employees via mail to be signed and returned. Not only does this added step cause delays, but the participation and rate of return on mailed applications is much lower than that of voice-stamped applications. Both employee and employer will appreciate the convenience and simplicity of voice-recorded signatures.

Before a telephonic enrollment, each employee is provided with an enrollment kit. The kit can be provided by the employer and often contains a letter from the employer that provides an overview of the enrollment process with an emphasis on the importance of speaking with a telephone representative. The kit can also be mailed to the employee's home, preferably in the employer's company envelope.

The enrollment kit should contain the agenda and an overview of the telephonic enrollment process, a description of the products and or programs available, and a worksheet that can be filled out by the employee before or during the call. Upon completion of the call, employees receive a confirmation of the product choices they made. This confirmation can be provided by the employer or sent directly from the call center to the employee via mail or email.

There are two types of telephonic enrollments: inbound and outbound.

Inbound Telephonic Enrollment

Employees participating in an inbound enrollment receive an enrollment kit that provides information about the products that are available and the agenda for the call. It also provides information about the enrollment "window," or the dates and times for them to call.

An inbound call can be set up in many ways. One approach is to assign each employee a specific time to call and speak with an enroller or benefit specialist. The second and most common method is to provide the dates and times of the enrollment window. For larger telephonic enrollments, the employee population can be scheduled to call by location or alphabetically. This is effective, as all employees are not trying to call at the same time and it reduces long wait times or the need to leave voice mails, which can frustrate the employee and employer.

Outbound Telephonic Enrollment

An outbound telephonic enrollment is similar to an inbound telephonic enrollment in that employees are provided with an enrollment kit and enrollment window. There are several ways to make outbound calls. One method is to assign each employee a scheduled time to receive a call from the enroller or benefit specialist. If the employer has many locations with few employees at each, the enrollment can be scheduled by location. For locations with multiple employees, an enroller can call a department or location on a specific day and time and speak to the employees individually, using the tag team method. A third option is for the enroller or benefit specialist to make multiple attempts to call the employees at different times and dates during the enrollment window.

Web-Based Enrollment

An increasing number of companies, especially larger companies, are looking to web-based enrollments as a way to allow employees to access their benefits information 24 hours a day. Web-based enrollments provide one location to review current benefits, make changes to personal data, review all benefits available and enroll in or change benefits at any time, at work or at home. This is becoming the method of choice for employers as it is the easiest and least disruptive to implement. However, this method yields a low participation rate and is not the method of choice for employees, who want to be educated about their choices and typically have questions.

Web-based enrollments for voluntary benefits are gaining popularity. Today, about half of all carriers offer web-based enrollment options, but they still have mixed feelings as this method has shown to yield low participation rates.

As web-based enrollments become more popular, they also need to become more employee-friendly in terms of needs analysis and enrollment ease. One option that is being explored and used by a few companies is web-based enrollments with an instant messaging application employees can use to ask for help. An enroller or benefit specialist is immediately available to answer questions via a pop-up window. A web-based enrollment portal can also be designed as merely a place for information gathering; with the actual enrollment completed telephonically.

Direct Mail

Direct mail marketing has been around for many years and is used by carriers as a way to provide product directly to employees or consumers. This method can be a cost-effective way to provide information to employees or consumers with little to no disruption to the employer. Direct mail can take the form of postcards or letters sent by mail, or it may be an email. The information provided by the direct mail piece should be creative to catch readers' attention and informative. Direct mail products can be self enrolled, where the customer fills out the application and mails it back. Or the customer can be directed to a website or given a phone number and enroll telephonically. The response to direct mail enrollments is typically under 10 percent and is the least preferred enrollment method.

The chart below illustrates the level of satisfaction and participation rates of employees for various enrollment methods:

Method	Participation
One-on-One	35-60%
Group Meeting	20-50%
Self-Enroll	10-25%
Telephonic	7-30%
Web	2-10%
Direct Mail	2-10%

Source: Eastbridge Consulting, Enrollment Practices 2006 Study

Enrollment Presentation

Historically, the delivery of worksite products or programs has been product-driven with an emphasis on product explanation and why the employee needs it. Unfortunately, one of the most common employee complaints about this method is the perception that it utilizes high-pressure sales tactics. This reaction leads to unhappy employees and, ultimately, to poor participation and persistency.

Rather than just supplying information, the employee communication strategy should present the information in an interesting, non-technical manner. The information should also be relevant to the employees. Employees should understand the material and it should make sense to them so they can take action.

Regardless of the enrollment method used, employees want education and choices based on their personal needs. The presentation should have all of the following:

- An introduction that states why the enrollment meetings are important to the employee
- An overview or agenda that explains what will take place during the meeting
- Education about the employer's current benefits offering
- Questions to help analyze and identify needs
- Explanation of the new benefits
- Education about how the benefits will meet employees' needs
- A discussion about deduction amounts
- Enrollment
- Review

Ultimately, in order for a voluntary benefit enrollment to be most effective and beneficial to an organization, it is important that all employees have the opportunity to participate in the process. Therefore, it is imperative to properly utilize a variety of enrollment methods based on the situation to ensure a successful outcome for everyone involved.

Chris Bernardine is the managing director of Employee Benefit Communications (EBC), a full-service benefits communications and enrollment company. EBC specializes in helping employers recapture lost benefit dollars by communicating with and educating their employees about the full value of their benefits, thereby helping them fully appreciate their total compensation. At the same time, EBC partners with insurance carriers, benefits brokers and employers to fight the rising costs of benefits by helping them expand and enroll their current benefits. This is accomplished with an extensive portfolio of products and services that can be purchased or enrolled at the worksite.

Chris has dedicated more than 15 years to benefit communication and employee benefits and is a past board member of the Mass Marketing Insurance Institute and current advisory board member of the Workplace Benefits Association as well as a national speaker on voluntary benefits, recruitment and retention and benefit enrollment.

Christopher Bernardine Sr., CES
Managing Director
Employee Benefit Communications
2701 N Rocky Point Drive, Suite 220
Tampa, FL 33607
Phone: 813-639-0099
Fax: 813 639-0098
Email: chris.bernardine@ebcfl.com
Website: www.ebcfl.com

Chapter Twenty

Enrollers – the Power Behind Employee Participation

ALICE GADDY-MEIER

CAROL LIST

RALPH RUSSO

To enroll is to engage somebody to enter – to envelope, to enwrap, to involve, to join. Therefore, an enroller is one who engages another to enter into, one who involves another...

Some view a voluntary benefit enrollment as a time to convince employees to buy something. Those who subscribe to this philosophy consider an enroller the person who facilitates this sales transaction. But, regardless of the enrollment methodology used, most enrollers view the enrollment process as an opportunity to connect with and educate employees. They see their role as a person who engages employees, entering into mini relationships with them, even for a brief 15 minutes. Enrollers are counselors who envelope and involve the employees, not only in the relationship process but also in the education of the product offering.

Although we interviewed 13 individuals, the rest of this chapter is devoted to the voices of several benefit counselors for their representative answers.

Overview:

Describe an enroller's responsibilities.

Alice - As enrollers it is our responsibility to communicate with employees. We must listen as well as educate, allowing them to make an educated decision about the products that make the most sense for their needs. Many enrollers spend most of the time talking and therefore do not hear what the employees have to say. As enrollers it is our job to not only communicate and educate, but also to counsel and help match products with the needs of the employees.

Carol – An enroller's responsibilities are as follows:

1. It is very important to understand the products you are selling.
2. Be professional and knowledgeable, but do not pressure clients.
3. Be a good listener and advise clients on their needs.
4. Call carriers to get answers to questions you are not sure of instead of assuming answers and making errors.
5. Complete the application and check for accuracy.

An enroller is professional, a good listener, answers questions, advises, sells and completes the application, making the clients comfortable and not pressured.

Ralph – An enroller's job is to educate and advise employees, based on the needs and financial capabilities of each individual.

Why are you an enroller?

Alice - I enjoy enrolling because I feel I am providing a service to the employees. Insurance is complicated as well as important. If employees do not understand the product, often they will not sign up for that simple reason. It is rewarding to know that insurance will be there when people need it the most. On the other hand, there is nothing more exasperating than to know that at the time one needs coverage the most, they will find out they do not have what they need.

Carol - I love what I do. I truly believe in what I do! I can relate to clients, as I have personal stories from my own life, which I share to help them relate to the needs. I feel I am not working, but rather helping clients and their families with their future needs.

Ralph – I chose to enroll for others versus owning my own company ·ause I have a greater opportunity to see more people and make a dif- ·e in their lives than I would organizing and running an office.

Training:

Is pre-enrollment training important?

Alice - Pre-enrollment training is very important. It is vital to the enrollment that the counselors are trained on the product and educated about how the enrollment is to be conducted. How can we act as counselors if we ourselves do not understand the products? When an employee comes to sign up, he or she is expecting to visit with a counselor who knows what they are talking about. I have been involved in enrollments for which we did not have any training, and employees can tell when an enroller is not prepared.

Carol - Yes, pre-enrollment training is vital, especially if the product is new. Also, computer training is important so the enrollment goes smoothly. The goal is to eliminate errors and problems on the actual enrollment.

Ralph - Absolutely. The employees of a company deserve to receive accurate information prior to making their decisions. Also, from a liability aspect, everyone involved in the enrollment process should be sure that the enrollers are thoroughly prepared with precise facts, resources, brochures, etc.

Who should provide your training?

Alice - For most cases, the enrollment companies provide the training. The training usually takes place a few days prior to the enrollment. Although on some enrollment occasions, no training was provided and I had to learn the products on my own.

If the enrollment involves core benefits, then it is the enrollment company's responsibility to train the enrollers. On the voluntary products side, a representative from the insurance company should do the training. As enrollers, we benefit the most when we have someone who deals strictly with that particular product do the training, as we're getting it straight from the expert's mouth.

Carol - I request training on a new product from a representative of the carrier. The carrier is responsible for training, as all products are a little different and the carriers are the only ones that know how they work. I always have lots of questions and need to know how it all works.

Ralph – Most of the brokers I work with do some training prior to each enrollment. However, it usually isn't enough. The broker or the person who owns the case should be responsible for training, whether it is through his or her office, the enrollment company or the insurance carrier.

It could be that several entities train for a specific enrollment. The enrollment company should teach the process, laptops, reports, etc. A carrier rep should teach the products. A member from the client company should come in to review their current benefits and help enrollers understand what the client wants to get from the enrollment. It is highly unlikely that any one person has the ability to train on all of these aspects.

What training methods do you prefer?

Alice - I enjoy a classroom environment. However, I learn the most when I am taught hands-on.

Carol - We request a meeting with a carrier representative who is knowledgeable about the products we are selling, as well as the computer program processes.

If possible, training should be done in person. However, I have done my own training prior to a case with information I've received. However, if enrollers are new, they definitely need one-on-one training. This eliminates questions and errors on the enrollment, makes the enrollment run smoothly, and the client feels the enrollers are knowledgeable.

Ralph – Training should take place immediately prior to the enrollment, using the exact same forms, products, procedures, etc. Training should be given to the entire group of enrollers at the same time, with plenty of opportunities to role-play and work one-on-one. In that way, enrollers can learn from each other, observe strengths and weaknesses within the team, and step in when needed to make the enrollment a success for everyone.

However, enrollers should have other ways to receive training throughout the year that is not specific to any particular enrollment. Enrollers should understand the nuances of the different forms of life insurance, for example.

What products require the most training and why?

Alice - I believe that core benefits certainly should be understood. I have been involved in enrollments where the enrollment company won the account because they stated that they would provide a service by enrolling the core benefits, and then did not train the enrollers on the core benefits. Therefore, the enrollers were not able to educate the employees. I felt that this was an injustice to everyone involved. Ultimately, the employees are the ones who have to make the decisions as to what plan best suits their families' needs, but as enrollers, we should have an idea as to what the plans are and how they work.

On the voluntary products side, the life products require more training because there are many differences between term, whole life and universal life.

Carol - Products that have lots of riders require the most training. Enrollers must understand all of them in order to explain them to the employees at the time of the application so they can choose what best fits their needs.

Ralph – Any products with heavier underwriting and potential claims issues require the most training. Employees need to understand all of the nuances of those types of policies so they are not surprised at claim time.

What products require the least training and why?

Alice - All products require training. Even though we may have sold particular products in the past, things change and we should be knowledgeable about current changes and trends.

Carol - Simple universal life policies require the least amount of training time.

Ralph – Life insurance is the easiest benefit to understand and explain. There are no problems at claim time – the person is either living or not. Plus, it's not a matter of *if* something will happen, as with a disability or critical illness policy. With life insurance, it's only a matter of when. Everyone has the need.

Enrollment:

What are your preferred enrollment methods and platforms?

Alice - I enjoy initial group meetings with one-on-one follow-up meetings to sign people up. The enrollment method that I enjoy the most when taking the application is the computer enrollment with the entire enrollment on one platform. There is nothing more frustrating than having to open many different screens while having to remember all of the different passwords. It is also an added bonus to have the forms pre-populated with the employees' information, as well as having the ability to print payroll-deduction forms on-site. The electronic signature is also a great tool.

I like to have brochures available when I am explaining voluntary products. If a brochure is nicely done, it aids in selling that particular product. A brochure adds a little more credibility because the employee actually sees the information in print.

Carol - I definitely prefer face-to-face, one-on-one meetings. Group meetings are most preferred in large companies, as all employees hear about products and ask questions at the same time. Enrollers must be very knowledgeable about product facts in order to answer questions at group meetings. After the meetings, it is preferable to meet with the interested employees one on one and face to face to enroll the actual products.

Ralph – Call me old fashioned, but I prefer face-to-face and one-on-one. It is the truest way to get to know someone in a short amount of time. In group meetings, it's always possible to get a heckler or a naysayer who instigates uneducated negativity among the crowd.

In your experience, which methods and platforms do employees seem to prefer?

Alice - Employees feel most comfortable when we keep it simple. Employees lose interest when we get really complicated. In addition, we do not look very professional when we are stumbling from one computer screen to the next and the employee and employer do not appreciate us taking too much of their time.

I have worked for enrollment companies that have enrollers go on site in pairs. That way, one person can be doing the selling while the other person can take care of the paperwork. I feel that when paired up, each enroller has more confidence, knowing that if one either forgets something or doesn't quite understand it, the other enroller may be able to help. I have had employees tell me that they like it when more than one person is doing the enrolling. They feel that there is more credibility to what the enroller is telling them, because they are not hearing it from one enroller, but from two who are telling them the same thing. It is very important to make sure that the enrollers work well together.

Carol – Employees prefer group meetings, then a one-on-one, face-to-face enrollment.

Ralph – Most employees seem to initially prefer group meetings, although I believe that after an effective enrollment process, employees would say they preferred face-to-face meetings. It gives them a chance to discuss their personal situations with someone who not only cares, but who also has some answers for them. You cannot get this attention in group meetings.

What products are you most comfortable selling and why?

Alice - I enjoy selling accident products. I like pointing out that the National Safety Council states that unintentional injuries are the fifth leading cause of death overall and the first among persons in age groups from 1 to 44. Even though we have major-medical supplement products to help with the out-of-pocket expenses that are not covered by health insurance, such as deductibles, co-payments and travel expenses, accident plans are an important piece of total coverage.

Cancer products are also very important. As advances in cancer treatment continue, more people survive. Meanwhile, living expenses such as mortgages, car payments and utility bills continue, whether or not one is able to work. With cancer indemnity products, the first-occurrence benefits can help when one needs it the most to fight the financial costs of cancer that are beyond the scope of traditional health insurance. And most employees understand disability products and ask for them, especially women of childbearing age, as they know that most disability products cover maternity leave. I have also sold lots of accident, cancer and critical illness products.

Carol – I feel comfortable selling all voluntary products and am always open to learn about new ones.

Ralph – I like to offer life insurance for the reasons stated previously. Everyone needs it. And even if people have life insurance, they usually could use more. It's an easy product to explain and therefore understand. Outside of the suicide clause, and after two years, the carrier will pay the claim with no questions asked, no doctor forms, no hassles. And critical illness plans make sense to most people simply because almost everyone has experience with family or friends with cancer and/or heart-related illnesses.

What products are you least comfortable selling and why?

Alice - I find life insurance a little harder to sell because most people do not understand the difference between term and whole life. There are a lot of differences between the permanent life products, such as whole life and universal life, and explaining those differences can become complicated. But all in all, I really have no comfort issues with any of the products. I know that as with everything, there is always going to be someone who finds fault with something, so as enrollers, we need to communicate with the employee and really listen so that we may help in matching the best product with that particular employee's needs.

Carol – None, as long as I am well trained prior to the enrollment.

Ralph – It's not that I am uncomfortable with the products, but I find the disability/medical family of products a bit time-consuming to explain. Things like coordination of current benefits, workers compensation, pre-existing conditions, doctor opinions, etc., make for a long presentation in order to explain them completely. However, I am a firm believer in those products and in fact, own some myself.

Ideally, products should be offered that make sense for the demographics of each particular enrollment. If the employees shun a certain product offering, perhaps it is not the right product for the group. Any time I have had a problem selling a product, it has been because the product was not a suitable choice. There are no bad products, just bad product selection.

Does product preference have more to do with the actual product and what it delivers, or the way it is bundled and marketed by the carrier?

Alice - I sometimes have a difficult time enrolling a certain product when I feel that product should not be offered in a particular case. Sometimes we are trying to sell products that are too expensive for what the employees make. It is also hard to sell a product that you don't believe in.

I like to see brochures that catch the employees' eyes. I enjoy seeing colorful, informative brochures that are easy to read and use layman's terms. Employees like to have something to carry away with them. It's like, "I bought something and I get something back in return."

Carol - Clients like to buy from a carrier they know and like to see a brochure/material about them. This can make a difference in a sale. Clients like to have something in hand to review.

Ralph – As with most things, presentation makes a big difference in how employees perceive not only the products, but also the enrollment as a whole. However, you can have the most beautiful brochure in the world and if the product is not right for the employee or employee group, the offer will be ignored. Proper product selection is paramount.

Does price make the sale? What else determines a decision to buy?

Alice - Price certainly does make a difference, but it is also the enroller's responsibility to create a need. I am not talking about pressure selling or overselling. Enrollers need to present the products in such a way that the employees leave with the feeling that they understand their benefits and that the enrollers assisted them to make the choices that best fit their needs.

Carol - Each client is different. Some look at price and others look at what is best for their future. As the enroller, you must get this feel from the client after asking them questions about their needs.

Ralph – Of course price does make a difference, but it is not usually the defining factor. If the need is there and the employee understands that the product offers a solution, the solution usually wins, as long as the price is reasonable. The enroller also must have the innate ability to connect with each employee so that the employee feels like they just got advice from a friend, and not a salesperson.

Does pre-enrollment employee education help you do your job?

Alice - It is important to have group meetings prior to the enrollment, in which the enrollment process is explained and products are highlighted. This relieves a lot of employee stress and gives employees a chance to think about the products and discuss the options with their spouse. When the employees arrive for the enrollment, they do so because the group meeting has piqued their interest.

Carol – Pre-enrollment education is very crucial. Education is needed in order to assess employees' needs and answer their questions.

Ralph – Pre-communication is a must. An employee needs to get as much information in as many formats as possible prior to the enrollment. It saves everyone a lot of time and employees can come to the enrollment with questions in mind.

How do you develop instant rapport and trust with employees, given the short amount of time you spend with them?

Alice - I have had to learn to listen. It is important to let the employees talk. When they feel comfortable, they will tell you a lot of what their needs and interests are. Being a good listener as well as a communicator is a key to a successful enrollment. I let people talk and maintain good eye contact.

Carol - I ask them some personal questions about their family and needs, and then share some personal stories of my own. Be a good listener and answer all of their questions with confidence and without any pressure to buy. I watch body language and listen to what they say. It's about being a good listener.

Ralph – I concentrate on them instead of me. I try to figure out what they need from me. Do they want me to be businesslike or friendly? Do they want to do all the talking or do they want to listen to a presentation? I try to hone in on their preferences. I watch and listen very carefully. When employees are ready to buy, I shut up, even if I'm only halfway through the presentation. Then, after filling out the paperwork, I review any important details I may have skipped. There's no use in talking on and on when they are ready to buy.

Are you there to educate, to sell or to do both?

Alice - I like to consider myself an educator. Although I realize that we need to sell, I also believe that there is a fine line between selling and being aggressive. I try to create a need, but I am careful not to be too forceful.

Carol – Both. Employees need to be educated and understand what they are buying.

Ralph – My first job is to educate. If the product offering is suitable to the audience, then an educated employee becomes a buyer. I try to learn about employees' unique situations to help advise them. I view myself as a facilitator between the employee's need and the products being offered.

Are you concerned about employees keeping their policies after the initial deductions?

Alice - Yes, I am concerned about people keeping their policies. But when we do our job right, and have educated and created a need and not oversold, we should not have to worry that employees will drop their policies.

Carol - Yes, that is why it is important to determine their needs up front.

Ralph – Yes. Even though I don't see what happens after an enrollment, I like to know that my time is well spent and that employees are better off after I leave.

How are enrollers important to the employer? What is your relationship with the employer and HR department?

Alice – Employees often view the enrollment company as a reflection of their employer. When the enrollers are professional and well trained, the employees see that the employer is making it possible for them to spend time with a professional who knows the products. This helps employees see the enrollment as another great benefit that is being provided by the employer.

Most enrollment companies request that enrollers not have any contact with the HR department. Typically, to avoid confusion, the enrollment company has one person who has direct contact with HR.

Carol - I talk directly with the HR department, as I am a coordinator/ enroller. I take them to lunch and develop a rapport with them, as they can make or break your enrollment.

Ralph –Employees view the enrollers as an extension of the employer. In that capacity, we must understand the corporate culture and conduct ourselves as one of the employer's team members.

Enrollers typically have little to do with the employer or HR department before and after the enrollment. The relationship usually exists during the enrollment and then only briefly, when questions or concerns arise.

Post Enrollment:

Describe your post-enrollment responsibilities.

Alice - I do not have any contact with the employees after the enrollment, unless I am called in the next year for the enrollment. Then I see familiar faces.

Carol - I send the HR staff a thank you for a great enrollment and advise them to call my office with any problems.

Ralph – Most enrollers move from job to job and have few post-enrollment responsibilities other than to turn in clean applications, reports, etc.

Is enroller continuity important? How often are you invited back to yearly re-enrollments?

Alice - It is important for employees to see the same faces. They get familiar with you and that builds trust. During annual re-enrollments, I have heard employees and employers complain when they see different faces. They are not comfortable with that.

I get called back to re-enroll probably 75 percent of the time. Sometimes I have to turn enrollments down because I have already committed to help with other enrollments. This happens most often in the fourth quarter when enrollment companies call at the last minute. Then I have to decide which enrollment to accept.

Carol – Definitely. Enroller continuity develops rapport, because clients feel comfortable speaking with the same enrollers. I usually get called back 100 percent of the time.

Ralph – Yes, because I don't see what happens to an enrollment on a day-to-day basis after the enrollment has concluded. It is nice to go back on an annual basis. The re-enrollment sales are easier because the employees learn to trust the same person. I get called back every year for re-enrollments. I know that the employees appreciate the continuity. After all, selling is about relationships.

These responses show that in a matter of moments, an enroller becomes a friend, a confidant and a trusted advisor who cares about the personal outcomes for people they may never see again. Good enrollers know how to quickly bring employees into this brief-but-meaningful relationship with them. This joining process leads employees to immediate decision-making and ultimately to a high level of participation in the benefit plans.

When enrollers and benefit counselors are trained under this definition, it's easy to understand how they become the driving force or the power behind a successful worksite enrollment.

Please contact the contributing enrollers via e-mail:

Alice Gaddy-Meier, alicemgaddy@yahoo.com

Carol List fantaseatc@aol.com

Ralph Russo, ralph_russo@prodigy.net

CHAPTER TWENTY-ONE

How Technology Can Substantially Increase Worksite Sales

JORDAN K. NADEL
PRESIDENT
FALCON TECHNOLOGIES, INC.

Since the early 1990s, people in meetings, agent's offices and insurance company home offices have repeatedly asked me one particular question: "Do electronic enrollments increase worksite sales?" After assisting numerous producers and insurance carriers for the past 11 years with over 1,000 enrollments, and insuring millions of employees, my response is a resounding "YES!" Not only do electronic enrollments increase case participation and profitability, but they also provide genuine value to the employer and employee.

This chapter will focus on how insurance carriers and enrollment firms can utilize electronic-enrollment technology to maximize their worksite marketing sales and dramatically improve their back-office efficiencies. The primary focus of this discussion will be traditional group and individual worksite products.

In 1998, we had the privilege of working with a major insurance carrier on a 750-life case in a small town in Georgia. The company manufactured jet engine turbine blades and employed a primarily blue-collar workforce. A well-known big box retailer was opening a store nearby and the employer was nervous about losing its workers to this marketing giant. The employer's insurance agent recognized the need to promote the company while supplementing its benefit package with voluntary benefits.

We worked with the insurance agent and employer to create a customized electronic benefit-communication program that detailed the employer's current benefit package and introduced the new voluntary plans. Employees reviewed a detailed customized benefit statement on a laptop, which clearly showed the value of their current benefit package (approximately 40 percent to 45 percent of their salary). To further communicate this value, the enrollers explained the hourly pay raise each employee would require in order to come close to matching the value of their current benefits package. The employees were then provided with a hard copy of the benefit statement to review at home.

Enrollers met with 92 percent of the employees, and more than $250,000 in annual worksite premium was written in that first year. More importantly, not one employee left the firm to work for the new competitor.

This example illustrates one way in which a technological solution was used to solve an employer's problem—and produce additional income for the agent.

In worksite marketing, it is critical that enrollers are provided favorable working conditions such as access to the employees in one-on-one meetings. The following are added value tools to offer an employer that can assist with gaining employee access and thus increased voluntary plan participation.

1. Full Core Enrollment: This is by far the most complicated method and entails the communication and enrollment of ALL of an employer's benefit plans, voluntary and statutory.
2. Beneficiary Cards: Many employers do not have accurate or current beneficiary information for their employer-paid life insurance policies. Favorable working conditions can be obtained when you do the work and collect and provide accurate beneficiary information.
3. Section 125 Plans: Many companies are not getting favorable participation in their Unreimbursed Medical and Dependent Childcare Accounts. This is typically because of poor communication, which can be easily corrected with a good enrollment strategy that includes individual meetings to explain the benefits of participation.
4. 401(k) Plan: Many employers are failing 401(k) discrimination tests. By communicating the benefits of a 401(k) plan, participation can be increased, discrimination testing issues can be eliminated and the door opened to discuss voluntary plans with employees.

5. Other ER Plans: My favorite plans to communicate are those that fall into the "other" category, such as the holiday turkey, uniforms, parking, paid time off and the company cafeteria. Most employees do not realize the cost of these benefits. Proper communication of the value of these benefits can increase morale and participation in voluntary programs.

Key Features of an Enrollment System

Before entering the benefits communication arena, one must make sure the enrollment system utilized can accommodate the needs of the employer, employee and enroller. The following are some questions to ask and some essential system features to look for:

Deployment time: How quickly can the case be implemented and deployed to the field? The industry standard for case deployment is two weeks for "voluntary benefit only" enrollments and four to six weeks for "full core" enrollments. For more complex core cases, the set-up time will increase.

Training: Does the vendor or insurance carrier assist with technical training for the enrollment team? What are the technical support hours? Even the best enrollment firms need training and technical support for the enrollment system and the insurance products. Technical support is not a nine-to-five job. The better vendors provide on-site and online meeting, web conferencing and video conferencing applications and training in conjunction with technical support. Enrollments occur when employees are at work, day and night, which means that enrollers will need technical support 24 hours a day. The following experience illustrates this point perfectly:

In 1998, we were assisting an insurance carrier with an enrollment of a company that manufactures seats for movie theaters. It was a relatively small company and the enrollment firm was using our system for the first time. In addition to providing on-site training, I offered Steve, the enrollment team leader, my cell phone number and told him not to hesitate to call if he had any questions or problems. The day after I left the enrollment, I was on my deck grilling dinner when my phone rang. My new friend Steve was calling and even though he had our documentation in front of him, he was having trouble synchronizing his enrollment data. I walked Steve through the process and not only was the task completed, but he learned how to complete the synchronization process and never needed additional assistance. When word got back to the carrier, our relationship was upgraded from "technology vendor" to "business partner." As a result, we went on to work with Steve on many other enrollments.

Ability to communicate and enroll an employer's "core" plans: This is one tool that can be used to achieve better working conditions for the enrollment team, which is the key to increasing worksite sales. The obvious challenge is that every employer's benefits are different and may require custom system coding in order to deliver the product. The responsibility of the technology team is to provide such customized systems.

Benefit statements/Election forms: Benefit statements and election forms are used in conjunction with core enrollments. Benefit statements illustrate the dollar value of an employer's core plans in a manner that is easily understood by the employees. Election forms reiterate the employee's benefit elections that have already been communicated by the benefits counselor.

Section 125 analysis: This tool allows the benefits counselor to illustrate the tax savings associated with paying for a voluntary benefit on a pre-tax basis. Of course, not all benefits are eligible for pre-tax deductions, and others may result in a taxable benefit to the employee. However, for those situations in which it is advantageous to deduct the premium on a pre-tax basis, the savings should be clearly communicated. In addition, many successful benefit counselors use the tax savings to encourage employees to purchase additional voluntary plans, which enhance the employee's benefits.

Needs-based tools: Some of the better enrollment systems contain basic-needs calculators which are used to provide employees with a rudimentary analysis of their financial situation and illustrate how purchasing a specified product can correct financial gaps. The needs-based calculators should focus on a specific point, be easy to use and concise.

Multi-carrier support for worksite products: In today's world of specialization, it is critical to offer employers the freedom to select the products that will most benefit their employees. Therefore, it is imperative that the enrollment system be able to accommodate multiple voluntary products regardless of the carrier. This sounds easy, but it can be very difficult to execute because most carriers use different enrollment techniques and back-office technologies. The best solution is to find a system that provides the widest access to a variety of carriers in addition to the services described in this section.

Synchronization process: This is the process of merging enrollment data and transmitting it from the laptop, call center or web system to the insurance carrier/third party administrator (TPA). In a traditional laptop enrollment, the data from all of the laptops are transmitted via a secure Internet connection to a central server. The information is then merged and made available for download to the enrollment team. Once downloaded, everyone's database is refreshed and each counselor has access to data for each employee. Now, employees can come back and meet with any counselor. On a scheduled basis, or once the enrollment has been concluded, the synchronized database is transmitted to the insurance carrier/TPA to begin the policy-issue process.

Reporting functionality: A solid synchronization process is the first requirement for providing top-notch management capability to the enrollment team. "Real-time" reports that summarize the case's production, as well as other pertinent information, are a must. The following are some of the reports a system should contain:

- Total enrollment production by product
- Production by product by enroller
- A "Not Seen" report detailing the names of employees (by location) who have not met with an enroller
- A report detailing how much time each enroller spent with each employee on a summary basis and by product
- A data extract of all deductions for the employer

Employer data feed: Once the enrollment has concluded, it is critical that the employer be provided with a report detailing the enrollment's results. It is best to review the desired format or system requirements with the employer prior to the enrollment to ensure a smooth data-transmission process. In addition, it is extremely important that one be able to generate the report without depending on a technology or insurance company for assistance.

Perpetual enrollments: Roughly 40 percent of the enrollments that utilize our system are "perpetual enrollments" that never end. These enrollments allow new hires and newly eligible employees to be enrolled in voluntary plans on an ongoing basis. In addition to providing a great service to the employer, perpetual enrollments provide the broker and enrollment firm with an ongoing revenue stream.

Ability to conduct re-enrollments: This process integrates the current underwriting offer with previously purchased policies and allows employees to purchase the maximum amount on a guaranteed-issue (GI) basis. If the employee elects coverage in excess of the GI amount, then the system automatically converts the new policy to a simplified-issue (SI) policy.

Insurance carrier/TPA efficiencies: The final step in the enrollment process is the transmission of the enrollment data to the insurance carrier/TPA. This is sometimes overlooked and is probably the most important feature of an enrollment system. Imagine working 12-hour days for three weeks straight. After you have enrolled 1,000 employees, you find out that it will take the insurance carrier two to three months to issue the policies and pay commissions because the applications have to be manually entered and imaged. An automated process takes a file produced by the enrollment system and seamlessly integrates it with the insurance carrier's administrative system, significantly reducing the "human factor" required to issue the business.

One of the carriers that utilize our services did a case study and found that it took 80 "person hours" to process 1,000 insurance applications vs. less than one "computer hour" to upload and image the same number of applications. And, the agent was paid within two weeks of transmitting the data.

5 tips for selecting an enrollment system

1. Test the System
   Prior to the enrollment, be sure to receive a fully functional demo version of the system you will be using. Test ALL aspects of the enrollment process and focus on the synchronization process, reports and especially the enrollment of voluntary and core benefits.
2. Beware of the "Vaporware" Salesperson
   This individual will have a very nice looking system with lots of pretty marketing screens, but it will lack any real calculation and application functionality. Look past the pretty pictures and focus on the details.
3. Look Out for the Server Person
   This is the person who proudly shows off his computer servers, which are either on the floor or in a closet in his office. Production

servers, which contain sensitive personal information, must be stored in a secured data-center facility. All production servers should be backed up nightly, with the backups stored at a different facility. The more high-end companies either co-locate at a data-center facility or have spent the money to build their own climate-controlled, fireproof room in their offices. All high-end data-center facilities have more than one type of Internet connection.

4. Check References
   Don't be afraid to ask for references from your technology vendor. You are trusting them with your client's sensitive data and you are obligated to do some due diligence.
5. Inquire About Encryption
   There are many aspects of the Health Insurance Portability and Accountability Act (HIPPA) and one of them involves data security. It is imperative that the enrollment system has at least one level of 132-bit data encryption. Additional levels may not be required by law, but the more levels of encryption, the better.

Where is enrollment technology headed in the future?

The days of one-on-one insurance sales over a kitchen table are over. Payroll deductions of premium for voluntarily purchased products have supplanted the antiquated system that dominated insurance product marketing for so long. The high-tech revolution enabled worksite marketing to not only become a reality, but also the norm. Electronic enrollment and benefit communication has nowhere to go but up. It is now. It is the future.

Jordan Nadel has more than 20 years of insurance industry experience in agency and home-office environments. In these capacities he has been involved with the development and implementation of numerous software solutions that have impacted many segments of the insurance industry. Jordan is the president of Falcon Technologies, Inc. and oversees the development and marketing of the company's electronic-enrollment and benefit-communication systems. Since 1997, more than $400 million of individual life insurance and health insurance premiums have been written using these systems.

From 2003 to 2004, Jordan served as the president of the Mass Marketing Insurance Institute, and has authored articles in national insurance industry publications on the subject of electronic enrollments. In 2007, he was honored with the Harlan Sher MI2 Member of the Year award for his numerous contributions to the institute. He and his wife Kathy have been married for 14 years and have three sons.

Jordan K. Nadel
President
Falcon Technologies, Inc.
565 East Swedesford Road, Suite 218
Wayne, PA 19087
Voicemail: 610-977-7502
Fax: 610-977-7519
Email: jnadel@falctech.com
Website: www.falctech.com

CHAPTER TWENTY-TWO

The Rewards of a Core Benefits Enrollment

H. CHRIS GUCKERT
MANAGING PARTNER
IMPACT ENROLLMENT SOLUTIONS

The key to any successful worksite enrollment is a complete understanding of the goals and objectives of everyone involved with the project. A core benefits communication strategy not only satisfies these needs, but also rewards everyone affected by the enrollment process. Employers gain assistance with their core benefit enrollment and are able to communicate in a positive way with their employees. Brokers, carriers and enrollment companies gain favorable access to the employees, who in turn enjoy a better education about their benefits, which means better understanding and better participation.

An experienced benefit communication and enrollment company assists a company's human resources department by:

- Providing education to employees to enhance and increase their awareness and appreciation of the benefits offered by the employer.
- Tying the education process to the existing core benefits package by providing a consolidated benefit-enrollment process.
- Enrolling multiple carriers and multiple products simultaneously, including voluntary payroll-deducted products.
- Utilizing customized enrollment software and professionally trained, salaried benefit counselors.
- Providing ongoing enrollment services and benefit administration

Who Wins with a Core Benefit Enrollment

Here's a look at an enrollment's four most visible players:

Brokers

Many brokers are presented with a worksite case by an existing client. These brokers may already have other benefits in place and are not actively soliciting worksite business. They recognize that if they don't consider supplemental benefits, they may lose the business to someone else. They also recognize the risk of having a third party conduct the enrollment and potentially ruin not just the worksite case, but also the entire client relationship. So, brokers risk losing the case if they don't enroll it or losing the case if they don't enroll it correctly. The broker can either walk away from the worksite opportunity or develop a trusting relationship with a quality enrollment company.

Because non-worksite brokers may not feel comfortable initiating, organizing and enrolling a worksite case, it can be difficult to approach an employer and say, "How about another life insurance plan?" But when brokers can provide their client with solutions for the enrollment process, they can often get a much more interested audience. It's easier for the employer to accept the idea of allowing full access to employees when they expect to receive a consolidated core benefit enrollment—especially when that enrollment includes the opportunity to clean up and collect employee data, provide electronic data transfer, offer benefit statements and educate employees, all at no cost to the company.

Employers understand that brokers cannot work for free and that this communication and education process is funded by the implementation of voluntary benefits. So what begins with employers looking to provide enrollment services at no cost to their company now includes their agreement to allow an enrollment company to meet with all of their employees and add supplemental benefits. This mutually beneficial situation allows brokers to meet with existing clients, and even prospective clients, without having to be a product pusher.

By aligning themselves with a competent enrollment company, brokers can focus on their core competencies and still reap the rewards of a successful benefit enrollment. Also, an enrollment company that has a strong relationship with the carrier may get better underwriting and concessions for both the broker and the client.

Employers

Often, management or members of an HR department decide to set up a core benefits-communication event and typically have two concerns. They know that the behavior of the enrollment company they select will directly reflect their judgment and they wonder, "Who are these enrollment people and what are they going to do when they sit down with our employees?" If the job is done poorly or incorrectly, the HR folks will look bad in the eyes of the employer and employees. They also are concerned about allowing employees to take time away from work.

Regardless of how ideal the case might appear or how interested employers may be in offering voluntary benefits, proper access to the employee population is crucial, and often difficult to achieve. Employers will become committed to the process when they realize the value of educating employees about their current benefits. When an employer understands how the enrollment will save time for their staff, consolidate and reduce forms, verify employee data and enroll all benefits, the request for access will be validated.

Employees

With today's employee benefits constantly changing and becoming more complex, the need to educate employees is ever increasing. Many times employees are handed large packets of information or referred to websites to gain information about their benefit plans. For many employees this is time consuming and very confusing.

By providing a core benefit communication and enrollment from a quality enrollment company specializing in this service, employees are able to meet or talk with professional benefit counselors, learn more about their benefit plans, and gain assistance with the enrollment process.

The end result is a better educated employee who is able to make better decisions about their benefit choices.

The Carriers

Carriers have something at stake, too. They need to align themselves with experienced, high-quality enrollment companies that will see close to 100 percent of the employees in order to get an even spread of risk. Most carriers are willing to offer better underwriting, better pricing and other concessions to an enrollment company that consistently delivers good participation and excellent persistency. That is why it makes sense for a carrier to underwrite the enrollment company instead of the broker. It's not the broker who is out there enrolling. The enrollment company is meeting with the employees, asking the health questions, and driving participation, which ultimately gives the carrier an even spread of risk.

Four Access Busters

The key to any successful enrollment hinges on the ability to meet with all employees. Because employers are often concerned about providing access to employees, it is important to understand how to overcome the objection. Employers need to feel comfortable with the enrollment process, understand the value added services available to them, realize the importance of employee education and communication, and admit their reluctance to designate their own internal staff to conduct a core benefit enrollment.

1. Getting Comfortable

The broker, employer and enrollment company should work in unison to develop a package that brings value to the employer. The goal is to make the employer feel comfortable throughout the process. That comfort level begins with the employer's understanding of the enrollment process.

The Employer Should Understand:

- In order to properly design, build and customize the enrollment campaign, the enrollment company and the enrollment team must have an understanding of the company's current benefits, company philosophy, open enrollment goals and objectives, and an understanding of the employee culture.
- Enrollers are highly trained and are not commissioned.
- Employees must be prepared for the actual enrollment process. This is achieved with various communication pieces, announcement letters and payroll stuffers.
- Scheduling employee meetings is not a cookie-cutter process. Within any organization there may be multiple means of scheduling employees such as sign up sheets prior to the enrollment, a tag-team approach or any other means that suit the situation. The ultimate goal is to see all employees and give them the opportunity to complete the enrollment process with the least amount of disruption to their normal daily activity. That means a lot of customized scheduling by department, by location, by shift, by nature of work and by availability. It's not a nine-to-five job.

When the employer becomes comfortable with the process and realizes that the primary focus is the enrollment and not the sale of a new product, the voluntary product offering becomes secondary.

2. Understanding the Value Added Services

The employer's decision-maker needs to know that the enrollment company is not just a product enroller. An experienced enrollment company should clarify this by explaining, "We're here as a communication company. We're going to spend a certain amount of time with your employees based on your goals. What can we help you do? Do you want an employee survey? Is there some information you need to pass out or collect?" These questions reassure the decision-maker that the enrollment team is there to facilitate the enrollment process. An enrollment that once began with non-mandatory meetings now becomes a mandatory process for all employees, simply because the employer has various vested interests in the process.

3. Realizing the Importance of Employee Education and Communication

Time is valuable to every employer. It can be extremely effective for an enrollment company, which typically spends 20 to 30 minutes with every employee during a core benefit enrollment, to ask the decision maker, "What is the likelihood that you or your HR department will have the time to sit down and talk one-on-one with each of your employees? Are the employees able to ask questions and get some answers right away?" These are particularly applicable questions for large, multi-location, multi-state employers. When the employer realizes the value of the time spent to educate and communicate with employees, obtaining access to those employees is no longer an issue.

4. Admitting Reluctance to Enroll

A lot of employers are willing to offer new benefits, but don't want to go through the enrollment process. This reluctance can be overcome by allowing an enrollment company to provide ancillary timesaving services.

Many employers, particularly larger ones, have invested a lot of time and money into online systems. Some of them are full-blown HRIS systems, while others simply provide online enrollment for core benefits. Often, an enrollment company can use the employer's online system to assist in the enrollment of core benefits.

The employer may worry that if benefit information is only available online, employees may not read it or be able to understand it. An experienced enrollment company can help the employer by providing education and assisting employees with the online system. Many employers will say, "We're just implementing the system and most of our employees don't know how to use the Internet, so just help us do this for the first year." The reality is that most of those clients will need help every year and so the employer, who now realizes the importance of providing yearly employee education and assistance, asks the enrollment company to come back and makes it mandatory for employees to show up.

Perpetual Enrollments Equal Perpetual Access

An increasing number of employers are requesting assistance with enrolling new hires. Specifically, they want the ability to allow new hires to enroll in voluntary benefits as they become eligible for core benefits. And so, providing ongoing or perpetual voluntary benefit enrollment services for new hires, either through face-to-face meetings, websites or call centers, is a growing service function. Coordinating the submission of new hires' data, for voluntary and core benefits, to carriers on a monthly basis has become the norm. The entire servicing process has changed from enrolling just once a year to an ongoing enrollment.

This valuable enrollment company function allows favorable access to employees and allows the enrollment company to function as a partner. Conversations with employees are about the benefits in general; worksite products naturally become a part of the process.

A Rewarding Conclusion

When employers hear the word "worksite", they often think about supplemental benefits. But a worksite enrollment is more than a mere product offering. A skilled enrollment company expands the process to include employee education and communication, along with the ability to enroll. When employees are informed, they make educated decisions. Once they understand how the voluntary benefits supplement their current plans, they are much more likely to participate and keep their coverage. When done properly, the core benefits-and-communication enrollment method helps make worksite better for everyone. Employers become long-term clients and gladly grant yearly access to employees. Persistency improves, which sustains underwriting privileges granted by carriers. And brokers are happy because their client is happy. And that's rewarding.

Chris Guckert began his insurance career in 1987. He managed and coordinated every phase of Aegon/Monumental Life Insurance's worksite division, including marketing, enrollment, product development and division management. As vice president of worksite marketing, Chris played a key role in the integration of several worksite divisions within Aegon, as well as the integration of Transamerica.

In 1999, Chris started Worksite Resource Group, a company that specializes in benefit communication and enrollment services. His experience and extensive knowledge of the worksite market has enabled the company, now known as Impact Enrollment Solutions, to become one of the leading enrollment firms in the country.

Chris speaks at industry related conferences such as MI2 and CLU, contributes articles to *Life Insurance Selling*, is an active advisory board member for several leading worksite carriers, participates in numerous industry related study groups, and has continued to be a leading producer for many major worksite companies.

H. Chris Guckert
Managing Partner
Impact Enrollment Solutions
4500 Black Rock Road
Hampstead, MD 21074
Phone: 410-374-3958
Fax: 410-374-1306
Email: cguckert@impactenrollment.com
Website: www.impactenrollment.com

Chapter Twenty-Three

Worksite Administration Best Practices

JAY PETTAPIECE
President
Vision Financial Corporation

MARION HOLLOWAY
Manager Client Relations
Vision Financial Corporation

Worksite administration is the ongoing service work that includes policy issue, billing, policyholder service and claims. Worksite administration also entails all of the work that occurs behind the scenes in preparation for an enrollment. Worksite administration typically takes place within the insurance carrier's home office. However, some carriers have outsourced all or part of their administration to third party administrators (TPAs) that specialize in worksite administration. In this chapter we will refer to both as the administrator.

Excellent administration is a key ingredient for a successful business model in the worksite market. It is the expectation of the producer, employer and policyholder that administration will meet each of their needs in a professional and effective manner. This expectation remains throughout the life of the case. By striving to meet these expectations, an administrator is essentially applying for the job every day. Anything less than well-administered business is a disappointment and a reason for the producer to reconsider his options.

Questions a producer should ask a potential administrator:

- **For how long have you been working in the worksite industry?**

  We believe that five or more years is an acceptable time frame. However, the real issue is the administrator's ability to demonstrate that its capabilities will meet your business needs.

- **Can you provide references from producers?**

  As the direct recipients of the results of administration, producers will have an opinion on the quality of service provided to their clients. An administrator should have and be willing to share those endorsements.

- **How many employer groups do you currently administer?**

  A client list of at least 300 to 500 employer groups demonstrates the administrator's ability to work with multiple groups.

- **How many policies are in force within your system?**

  The number of in-force policies will be driven by the size of the groups that the administrator is working with. There is no magic number that will determine the capabilities of an administrator. However, if there are more than 50,000 in-force policies, this is a good start.

- **What is the typical size of the groups you administer?**

  An administrator likely has flexibility in its capabilities if it is working with groups of varying sizes with multiple payroll frequencies.

- **Can you accept electronic enrollment data or electronic premium payments from employers?**

  Though much of the insurance industry still relies on paper, more and more aspects of the business are moving to electronic enrollment and payment. In order to provide service to meet all needs, an administrator should be able to provide both electronic and paper administrative options.

Worksite administration is a linear process. If the initial steps are incorrect, the remainder of the process will be problematic, perhaps for the entire life of the case. The following six points highlight these worksite administrative processes.

1. Case Set-Up

To be successful in worksite marketing, the administrator must pay attention to detail before, during and after the enrollment. The administrator's case set-up process should be a proactive one that ensures the administrative details for the case are set up properly prior to the enrollment so that when the applications are received in the administrative office, the underwriting and contract-issue processes will flow smoothly and efficiently.

The role of the producer in the case set-up process is that of facilitator. Notification of new cases should include the following:

- Employer name
- Employer contact information
- Number of employees
- Other voluntary products the employer has offered
- Case underwriting criteria
- A case census, if required
- Expected enrollment dates and any subsequent changes

When the case set-up process is complete, the administrator then assesses the requirements and expectations regarding deductions and billing. It is important to note that the administrator should allow the producer to be as involved as is necessary or required by the producer's business model. Some producers prefer a "hands-on" approach and will introduce the administrator to the employer payroll contact. They may also participate in conversations about the case via conference call. Other producers prefer to give the administrator control over the entire process. They simply make the introduction to the employer payroll contact and then step away from the process. Either approach can be effective so long as time is spent prior to the enrollment to determine the employer's deduction and billing needs. We will expound upon the importance of deduction administration later in this chapter.

Incorrect deductions and inaccurate billing can undermine even the best and most successful enrollment. If the administrator is able to work proactively with the employer to set up deductions and billing prior to enrollment, that effort will pay off for months and years after the initial enrollment.

Situation: How a Good Case Can Go Bad

A common error is neglecting to verify that payroll frequency is the same as the employer's deduction frequency. Often, an employer has 26 pay periods per year but only makes deductions 24 times per year. If the administrator does not verify that the payrolls and deductions follow the same frequency, an employer with bi-weekly (26) payrolls that deducts only 24 times per year will have incorrect deductions. Insufficient premium will be collected and it can take months to rectify the situation. When case set up has been done correctly, payroll deductions will not be a problem.

To illustrate:

For an application submitted with a $5.00 weekly premium, the annual premium is $260.00 If the employer has a bi-weekly payroll and deducts each time a payroll occurs, the bi-weekly deduction will be $10.00

If, however, the employer pays its employees 26 times per year but only deducts for voluntary benefits two times per month, the semi-monthly deduction will be $10.83. In this case, if the only question asked of the employer during the case set up was about the frequency of the payroll, and if the actual frequency of deductions was not identified, the payroll deductions for the participants will be incorrect.

2. New Business:

The administrator should have a designated staff to receive applications from each enrollment. This department should verify that submitted information is accurate and begin the new-business process. The administrator should be able to quantify the number of applications received from an enrollment and track each application accurately until it is issued or reaches a different conclusion such as cancellation or declination.

Time is of the Essence

Typically, an issued policy is the only tangible evidence that an insured employee receives in exchange for the deductions that are coming from his or her paycheck. Therefore, it is important for the administrator to issue and mail policies as close as possible to the first payroll deduction date. The producer can help to achieve this outcome by conducting the enrollment according to the underwriting parameters approved for the group and by completing the applications accurately. This will enable the administrator to conduct the new-business process efficiently and effectively.

A common misstep for producers is to hold applications for an extended period of time in order to scrub the applications prior to submission. By holding on to the paperwork, the time frame required by the administrator for processing is extended, which can delay the policyholder's receipt of the issued policy. The more time it takes for the applicant to receive an issued policy, the more likely it is that the policy will not be accepted by the insured. Many of the qualifying questions on applications are related to a particular time frame. In a worst-case scenario, applications that are held for too long in a producer's office can be outdated by the time they are submitted because the answers to qualifying questions have become invalid as time has passed.

An administrator should provide specified measurements regarding the time required to complete all necessary functions, including policy issue. Typically, an administrator should be able to underwrite, issue and mail policies within 30 days of receipt of the completed applications or electronic enrollment data.

Many aspects of worksite enrollments have changed from what was once a paper process to an electronic one. Many employers have a workplace that can support on-site electronic enrollment on laptop computers. Electronic applications typically result in policies being issued faster than paper applications. However, some workplaces do not have the resources to support electronic enrollments. Therefore, it is important that the administrator be able to support both electronic and hard-copy enrollments.

3. Deductions, Billing & Collections:

Policyholders expect that premium will be paid from the monies deducted from their paychecks, and both policyholders and their employers expect those deductions to be accurate. Though the billing and collections process ends with reconciling and allocating paid premium, the most critical administration occurs before the receipt of premium payment from the employer. Proper case set-up will ensure that this is done successfully.

It is very important to pay attention to "rounding". If the initial deductions submitted to the employer are rounded differently than in the administrator's system, the employer may end up with penny errors on every individual on the list bill. Employers who have been told during the sales process that worksite benefits are easy to administer will not be pleased with penny errors.

The Importance of Rounding:

A common method of calculating payroll deductions is to annualize the weekly premium and divide by the number of deductions to be taken based on the employer's payroll system. There are a few different methods of rounding the results of the deduction calculation, most commonly rounding up or rounding near. It is important for the employer or producer to match the administrator's method of rounding to ensure the accuracy of employees' deductions.

For example: A weekly deduction of $8.54 will result in an annual premium of $444.08. For an employer with a semi-monthly (24x) payroll, $444.08 divided by 24 will result in a payroll deduction of $18.50333333.

If the administrator rounds near the actual payroll deduction, the deduction will be $18.50. If the administrator rounds up it will be $18.51.

A penny does not seem to be a large difference on an individual payroll deduction. However, if every deduction is off by one penny in a group of 1,000 employees, the administrator may have to manually adjust the payment of every premium, even if no deductions are missed and the premiums are paid as billed electronically by the employer. What could have been a simple upload and reconciliation can become a lengthy manual process that delays the premium posting process, which may affect a claim. The timely generation of commission payments can also be affected.

The initial deduction must be taken correctly and every payroll deduction thereafter must be correct as well. This requires the administrator to communicate changes (additions, changes and terminations) to the employer in a very timely fashion, so that the employees' deductions are current and accurate at all times. If the producer is handling communications directly with the employer in the "hands-on" method, the administrator should be able to provide change data directly to the producer.

Premiums should be reconciled quickly for two reasons:

- To assure that policyholder service or claims that might occur during a given month will reflect the premiums that were paid
- Because commissions are not paid until premiums are allocated

4. Commission Payment:

The administrator's commission processes must ensure that commission payments are generated accurately. Here are some things to look for:

The commission statement and data must be user friendly. Commissions should be tracked by case. The producer should be able to readily assess:

- The policy numbers as well as the employee and insured's names
- The amount of commission that is earned at a policy level
- How commissions have been affected by terminations and lapses
- The payback of advanced commissions

The administrator should be able to pay commissions at least twice per month. Employers pay premiums throughout the month even if all list bills are due on the first of the month. Therefore, commissions paid more frequently than monthly allow for better cash flow for the producer. Additionally, commission payments should be available in check form or via ACH as requested by the producer.

5. Customer Service:

Ultimately, the policyholder is everyone's customer. The carrier, administrator, producer and employer each have a responsibility to provide a consistent, equitable service to all policyholders. The policyholder must have a positive experience during each service encounter with the administrator. All service requests, whether written or verbal, should be provided promptly, efficiently and courteously. The administrator should be able to provide multi-lingual service when required. All customer service staff should be fully trained in all products for which they are responsible to answer questions. This can be as broad as explaining a product to a new policyholder who is uncertain about the benefits the policy provides or as specific as explaining the policy language to a policyholder.

All transactions should have measurable standards for turnaround that the policyholder can depend upon. For example, a life-insurance administrator should have specific time frames for the processing of a surrender, a loan or a beneficiary change.

Telephone calls should be returned within one business day. Simple transactions such as address changes or beneficiary changes should be completed within three business days. More complex transactions, such as financial transactions, should be completed within 10 business days.

6. Claims:

The claims process is often the administrative "moment of truth" for the policyholder, when he rightfully wonders if all of those premium deductions will provide for his needs. The administrator must recognize that an insured's claims experience is likely to be emotionally charged. Not only does the administrator need to gather detailed information at this time, but also administrative responses to requests from the claimant must be made in a sensitive and understanding manner.

Prompt settlement and payment is essential for death claims for life-insurance policies sold at the worksite. Turning a death claim payment around in two week's time was critical to a 40-year-old beneficiary who lost her 45-year-old husband to an unexpected heart attack. The family did not have savings to fall back on, so quick payment of the death benefit ensured that the funeral expenses were covered and that the widow had funds to pay other bills. As a result, instead of spending her time worrying about how she was going to make ends meet, the widow could devote time to helping her son and daughter cope with the loss of their father.

The Results of Good Administration

Worksite administration is a linear process. If the initial steps are incorrect, the remainder of the process will be problematic, perhaps for the entire life of the case. Conversely, if the administration is performed correctly, a case can run smoothly indefinitely. Although the initial enrollment is critical, ongoing re-enrollments are also affected by the quality of administration. The annual re-enrollment revenue for worksite business should be approximately 20 percent of the initial enrollment revenue. Therefore, it is critical that a case be administered correctly so that it can be a source of revenue for many years.

Ultimately, a successful worksite strategy results from a partnership between sales and administration. Good communication and an understanding of each role ensure a successful long-term relationship and that thousands of employees and their families, whose lives are improved by the products offered, will benefit for years to come.

Jay Pettapiece co-founded Vision Financial Corporation in 1989. When forming this company, Jay drew from his distinguished career in the insurance industry as well as his experiences as senior vice president of marketing for Maine Fidelity Life Insurance Company, one of the best service organizations in the worksite industry. Jay is a career insurance executive who knows the payroll deduction business from every perspective. He spent 15 years in various field management positions for Aetna Life and Casualty and was vice president of mass marketing at Liberty Life Insurance Company prior to joining Maine Fidelity Life. Jay has served on the Greater Keene Chamber of Commerce board of directors and is their past president.

Jay is also past president of the Mass Marketing Insurance Institute and was presented with the Ancy Pinnacle Award for his distinguished service to the insurance industry in 2007. He was inducted into the Benefits Marketing Worksite Marketing Hall of Fame in 2005.

Jay Pettapiece
President
Vision Financial Corporation
17 Church Street
P.O. Box 506
Keene, NH 03431
Phone: 1-800-793-0223 ext. 207
Fax: 603-357-0250
Email: jpettapiece@visfin.com
Website: www.visfin.com

Marion Holloway has more than 17 years of worksite marketing experience with Vision Financial. She began her career as a case coordinator and later became the supervisor of the case coordination department. In 1998, Marion moved into her current position as manager of client relations. In this role, she serves as a primary contact for the company's insurance carrier clients and contributes to the company's marketing initiatives.

Marion Holloway
Manager Client Relations
Vision Financial Corporation
17 Church Street
P.O. Box 506
Keene, NH 03431
Phone: 1-800-793-0223 ext. 206
Fax: 603-357-0250
Email: mholloway@visfin.com
Website: www.visfin.com

Chapter Twenty-Four

The Service Samba

DC REDIC
President
DC Redic, Consulting

(This story is true. Only the names have been changed to protect the innocent.)

The phone rang.

Our agency sells accident, disability, major illness, life and long-term care insurance to the worksite market. We choose to enroll, to re-enroll and to "service what we sell." This strategy provides continuity to our policyholders and a known, reliable resource to our employer clients.

I glanced at the Caller ID: "Matusek, Amelia."

I sipped my coffee. Over the years, we have found that 90 percent of our customer-service work is generated by an identifiable 10 percent of our client base. Amelia Matusek is one of those select few.

The phone rang a second time. I was alone in the office that morning running updates on our network. My name is Creed. I took the call.

"The Workers' Insurance Group, Daniel Creed speaking."

"This is Amelia Matusek."

"Good morning, Mrs. Matusek."

"I'm not a Mrs. anymore, so don't call me that."

"I see." Apparently a 'qualifying event' had occurred. I asked the obvious question, "So, should I offer you my condolences or my congratulations?"

"Congratulations. The legal proceedings ended six months ago and you people owe me money." Amelia was never one to beat around the bush.

"We owe you money?"

"Yes, you owe me money. I've been paying for accident coverage on my ex-husband since the divorce and I want my money back."

I keyed "Matusek" into my database. "Your former husband's name is Edward?"

"Yes."

"And you have three children?"

"Yes."

"Agnes, Andrew and Archie?"

"Correct."

"Looking at your policy information, Amelia – may I call you Amelia?"

"I guess."

"I see that your cancer coverage is for an individual – just you – but your accident-disability policy is a family policy."

"So?"

"The premium you're paying for the accident coverage is for your immediate family. There is no difference in the premium amount if you have one husband and three children on the policy or no husband and 20 children on the policy. The premium is a family premium regardless of the number of insured."

"The premium won't change?"

"Correct. I also see that you have filed a number of accident claims over the past five years."

"Well, I was in a car wreck – broke my leg and missed a month of work. Archie broke his arm at school. Agnes fell down the stairs – split her head open and cracked her collarbone. Edward, my ex, ruptured a disk shoveling snow."

"Those claims were all paid?"

"Yeah, they were."

"So, you're happy with the coverage?"

"They did pay the claims."

"And you want to keep the coverage. The children are still in your care?"

"Yeah, I guess, but I want Edward's name off the policy."

"That's easy enough. You can call the insurance carrier directly or I can send you a service form. You'll need to fill in the policy number, the name to be removed, sign it and mail it in."

"Send me the form. I can't spend all day on the phone. My shift starts in 15 minutes and no one is ever in their office at this hour of the morning."

"You could download the form from the carrier's web site."

"Send me the form."

"I'll put it in the mail this morning."

"And put the policy number on it."

"No problem."

"What about my life insurance?"

"You have two policies on yourself. The first was issued four years ago; the second was issued last year. Each policy has a $50,000 face amount. Edward is the only beneficiary listed."

"We need to change that."

"I'll send you the forms – one for each policy."

"Fine."

"And you have a life policy on Edward."

"Aha!"

"Aha?"

"I knew you people owed me money."

"I'm sorry, but I don't..."

"I canceled that policy."

I scrolled through Amelia's data on the monitor.

"I don't see any cancellations in your file."

"I told that girl."

"Which girl?"

"Your girl, your what-do-you-call-her, your enroller. Four months ago."

"Let me check." I clicked through four more screens. "I see, now."

"You see what?"

"All of our enrollers take notes during their meetings with the employees. Veronica Gripp, the enroller you spoke with, made a note that you mentioned canceling your husband's policy."

"I told you."

"Veronica also noted that she told you we needed a release form with your signature before we could cancel anything. Do you remember?"

"I don't know, she may have mentioned something about a form."

"Do you remember signing a release form?"

"Who has time for that?"

"Amelia, we have specific procedures in place to avoid 'misunderstandings.' We cancel no one's coverage until we have a signed release form in our possession. Human resources has the forms and they are very diligent about crossing Ts and dotting Is. Once the form is signed and dated, HR faxes the document to our office where it is scanned into the database. In fact, any piece of paper that moves into, out of, or through this office is scanned into the database."

"So I need to talk to HR."

"To cancel a policy, yes."

"What about the premium deductions?"

"HR immediately notifies payroll to stop the appropriate deductions. Then payroll calls us to confirm."

"You're efficient, Creed, I'll say that for you."

"*Thorough* is my middle name."

"You couldn't cancel a joint credit card for me, could you? That's next on my list."

"Sorry, Amelia, we don't do credit cards. Any other insurance issues this morning?"

"Maybe – hey, Betty, I've got this guy from The Workers' Insurance Group on the phone. He seems to know what he's talking about. You wanna ask him about that lapse notice? What? No, I'm not going to throw you the phone. You'll drop it. Come over here – and I wouldn't eat those scrambled eggs if I were you. Houston to Thoroughgood, you still there?"

"Always."

"O.K., here's Betty."

"Betty who?"

"Hello, hello? Is anyone there?" asked a voice that was not Amelia's.

"This is Daniel Creed with The Workers' Insurance Group."

"You're the insurance man?"

"I am the insurance man, and you are?"

"Betty. Betty West. I work with Amelia."

I keyed "West, Betty" into the database. "Good morning, Betty. Did I hear Amelia say something about a lapse notice?"

"I don't want to be a bother, but I think someone made a mistake."

"Tell me what happened."

"Well, I took out a life insurance policy and an accident policy the first year your company visited us."

I looked over the information on the computer screen. "Yes, both of those policies were issued six years ago, now."

"And the hospital has been taking $8.72 from my pay every week and sending it to the insurance people. I always look at my pay stub to make sure."

"O.K."

"And in all those years, I've never missed a week. Then, when I got home from work yesterday, there was a letter from the insurance company saying that I owed $23.60 in back premium and that if I didn't pay by the end of the month, the policy would lapse."

"$23.60?" I did a quick calculation, and $23.60 divided by $8.72 did not equal an integer.

"I don't know how they got that number," continued Betty. "I don't know how they got a number at all. I never miss work. I never even take vacations."

"Were any policy numbers on the notice you received?"

"I don't remember. I left the papers at home."

I pulled up Betty's application. "Your life insurance premium is $4.00 per week. That doesn't work with a bill for $23.60. Your accident premium is $4.72 per week ... and that divides $23.60 exactly five times. That's it."

"That's what?"

"The bill is probably for five weeks of accident premium. Let me make a phone call to check on this."

"Jane, Sandy, Liz, Kelly, Ann, Mike and Frank all got letters, too. Do you want to talk to them?"

"Where are they?"

"They're sitting here looking at me. We're in the cafeteria."

"I'll talk with them in a bit. Can you hold for three minutes while I make a quick call to the insurance carrier?"

"I guess, it's your 800 number, but don't be too long, our shift starts in 10 minutes."

"Okay, Betty, I'll be right back."

I pressed the "Hold with Music" button, then the "Line 2" button and dialed the carrier.

"You have reached the Extensive Insurance Company's automated agency telephone system. To continue in English, press one..."

I pressed "one."

"If you know your party's extension..."

I pressed "7 – 4 – 3" without much hope of anyone answering.

"Accounting," said a tired voice I recognized.

"Good morning, Marlene."

After a second's pause, "Daniel Creed, is that you?"

"The very same."

"Why are you calling at ten to seven in the morning?"

"Why are you working at ten to seven in the morning?"

"You shouldn't answer a question with a question."

"Busy?"

"You don't know the half of it, but that's my problem. Now, what's your problem?"

"Who said anything about a problem?"

"At this hour of the morning, it's always a problem."

"Well, since you asked, a flock of lapse notices landed on a big client's employees yesterday afternoon, and I was wondering..."

"Case number?"

"729762."

"That hospital in Texas?"

"Yes, Ma'am."

Marlene sighed, "Here we are... 39 lapse notices were issued Monday morning for that case."

"39?"

"Thirty-nine. Let me look at the policy numbers real quick. They all end with a two or a four."

"All accident or major illness policies. No life policies?"

"No life policies. Hmm, this is odd..."

"What?"

"They all missed exactly five weeks of premium, every last one of them."

I clicked over to Betty's payment history for the past 12 months.

"You're right. Betty missed five straight weeks of premium starting May 1."

"Betty?" asked Marlene.

"Betty West."

"She's on my lapse list."

I had a hunch. I clicked back to Betty's original application. There it was, staring me in the face.

"Marlene, can your software pull up the occupations of everyone on that list?"

"I think so, hang on a second... Let's see... Here we go... and they're all nurses, including your..."

"Betty West. Could you check a couple of their payment accounts – when was premium missed?"

"No problem. Liz McKenna missed five straight weeks of premium starting May 1. Frank Dorazio missed five straight weeks of premium starting May 1 – so did Kelly Shea. There seems to be a pattern emerging. Why would they all miss five weeks of premium starting on the same day?"

"That's the day all the nurses went out on strike."

"For five weeks?"

"For exactly five weeks, so that answers that question. Could you..."

"...send you a list of the affected policy owners?"

"You read my mind."

I heard a burst of keyboard clatter.

"Check your email."

I clicked the mailbox icon.

"Got it. Marlene, you're my hero."

"Sweet talker."

"I have to run, Betty's on hold and her shift starts in a couple of minutes."

"Do you folks still play that bossa nova music when you put someone on hold?"

"Yep, everyone seems to like it. We also have some big band cuts."

"I like the sambas. I'll have to get George to take me dancing one of these nights when the world isn't crashing down."

"All work and no play..."

"Truer words were never spoken."

"I'll talk to you, Marlene."

"Later."

I pressed "Line 1."

"Betty, are you still there?"

"I am."

"I spoke with the insurance company and that bill is for five weeks of missed accident premium."

"But when?"

"Remember the nurse's strike?"

"Oh, the strike, I didn't even think about that. I was here every day, but I wasn't at work, I was on the picket line. I won't lose my insurance, will I?"

"No, not at all. Just pay the bill and you'll be up to date."

"What about my life insurance?"

"The life insurance is a different animal. It's what's called a universal life policy. It builds up some cash value as the months go by. That way, if you miss a payment or two, the policy automatically uses some of that cash to pay the premium. Your policy is six years old and would have enough of an internal reserve of cash to pay the $20. Now, if you want to be absolutely safe, you should send the insurance company a check for that $20 with a note telling them it's for the missed premium. That way, all the values will be back to normal."

"What about Jane and Sandy and the rest of them?"

"I'll send human resources a list of the folks who received those lapse notices. They're all nurses who have accident or major illness policies. They can either call here to confirm the amount they owe or check with HR."

"I'll be sure to tell them that. And thank you for helping. I was worried."

"Betty, you're welcome. If you ever have any questions or concerns, just call. I can't help if I don't know there's a problem."

"Can I ask one more question?"

"Certainly."

"What was that music you played when I was on hold?"

I glanced at the playlist. "That was Sergio Mendes's version of *So Nice*."

"Well, I thought it was very nice. Oh, Jennifer's waving. I think she wants to talk to you."

"Well, put her on the phone and I'm glad you liked the music."

"Here she is," said Betty.

"Hello, hello, this is Jenny James."

"And I'm Daniel Creed."

"Oh, hello Daniel. Since everyone else was talking to you, I thought I might too. I have a question about my coverage."

"Ask away, Jenny."

"Well, after all these years, I'm finally going to retire."

"You sound excited about that."

"I am. I get to spend more time with my grandchildren and I'm so looking forward to that, but I was wondering about my insurance. I think the lady I spoke with last year said I could continue the coverage even after I left work here."

"You have a major illness policy and three life insurance policies. They're all portable, so you can take the coverage with you when you retire."

"How do I do that?"

"We set up accounts with the insurance companies so that you will be billed at home or you can have the premium paid automatically from your checking account."

"Will it be more expensive?"

"Not at all. You'll have the same coverage at the same cost. When do you plan to retire?"

"In two months."

"Here's what you need to do: Decide if you want to be billed at home or use the bank draft service, then, two weeks or so before your last day, give me a call and I'll get the ball rolling. You'll need to fill out a few forms to give the O.K. for the billing to start. I can walk you through that when the time comes."

"That's all?"

"That's all."

"I don't want to miss any payments or anything."

"You won't, Jenny. We'll take care of you."

"You've been very helpful, Mr. Creed. And I... Uh oh, Amelia's giving me one of her looks. I think she wants her phone back."

"Remember, call me two weeks before your last day."

"I will. Here's Amelia."

"Danny Boy, are you still there?"

"Like I said before, Amelia, I'm always here."

"You've put in a full day's work already."

"It's part of the job."

"Well, our job starts in exactly two minutes, so no one will bother you until 10 o'clock."

"What happens at 10?"

"Coffee break."

"Ah, yes, coffee break."

"We'll be talking to you, Danny. Got to go." Click.

The phone line went dead. The dial tone kicked in. I pressed "Line 2," dialed our office's 800 number, put myself on "Hold with Music," switched to speaker-phone, selected the Quincy Jones cover of *Blues in the Night*, and poured another cup of coffee. The day was young.

DC Redic, an electrical engineer and licensed insurance agent, has worked with computers since 1971. He has served as a consultant to, and written software and training manuals for, engineering, real estate and insurance firms for more than 30 years. He has also taught the fine art of software manipulation at corporate and career training centers, and produces the highlight film for the local high school basketball team each year.

DC Redic
President
DC Redic, Consulting
dcredic@prodigy.net

CHAPTER TWENTY-FIVE

Believe in Re-Enrollments

MARK PETRO
PRESIDENT
MARK PETRO AND ASSOCIATES

The Market

Early in my insurance career, I saw tremendous potential in the worksite arena. As a former manufacturer's representative for a major food company, I had many close contacts in the wholesale grocery business. I realized that these decision makers could be put to immediate and profitable use. Eventually, supermarkets and then nursing homes became my marketing niche because I felt that food and medicine were fairly recession-proof industries. And it's been a good call. One of my long-standing supermarket accounts operates 50 locations with an average of 80 employees per store. This size provides a combination of employee turnover and stability that makes it a good place to sell life insurance to the new hires and existing clients annually, based on their needs.

A Different Business Model

Because of these relationships, re-enrollments are imperative to the success of my business. Like many others who specialize in the worksite arena, I close and enroll new companies each year. But unlike most, I re-enroll the majority of those cases myself on an annual basis. Over the years, I have found that employees want two things from their insurance agents: service and rapport. They expect to be appreciated and not to have their business taken for granted. They want some connectivity with a person who will be there year after year, someone they get to know. When employees see me every 12 months, they realize that I'm dedicated to the job and committed to helping them achieve future financial security. Long-time employees who haven't yet bought insurance say,

"Hey, maybe he's a pretty good guy. I hear good things about him and he keeps coming back. I should talk to him." And when impressionable new hires see that their associates and friends do business with me, they are more willing to listen to what I have to say.

While re-enrollments are significant to employees, employers also appreciate that the initial enrollment is not a one-shot deal. They want someone to service their existing employees and to meet with their new hires on a regular basis. This ongoing service solidifies my relationship with the employer and also improves employees' perception of their employer.

For companies with high employee turnover, an annual re-enrollment is warranted and can be profitable. If a company doesn't have much turnover, it is still worth going back, but perhaps every second or third year. Even in a business that has stable employment, it is important to remain in contact with the employer. Throughout the year, I stay in touch via letters, emails, and telephone conversations to ensure they are kept up to date on policy service activity, new product offerings and to prevent infiltration by a competitor.

Re-enrollment Day

A re-enrollment is different from an initial enrollment and requires an additional set of paperwork. I bring the usual forms, such as brochures, applications and beneficiary forms. To help with the review process, a vital part of every re-enrollment, I have also created an "interview worksheet" that is a summary of each employee's current coverage. This review sheet reminds the employee of his or her coverage and how it works by illustrating the current death benefit, the approximate cash value at age 65 and any attached riders. The worksheet also has a place for names, addresses and general contact information, as well as marital status, current beneficiaries and additional policies.

Every year, as I meet one-on-one with each employee, I take notes on the interview worksheet. Does the employee have a child in the military or a spouse who travels a lot? Is adequate coverage in place? I'm trying to better understand each situation so I can find possible holes or hot buttons and recommend appropriate solutions. The interview worksheet also helps to soften the sales process. I'm seen not as a solicitor, but as a friend who is genuinely interested in reviewing the situation and making requested changes.

The main goal of the presentation is to establish credibility. To achieve this, I talk about my other clients that have already implemented the program. I also use the "me too" approach to help build credibility and push along the sales process. So, I might say, "If someone in your department has a policy, you should consider one too. If your manager is a client of mine, maybe you should be too."(This is said only with the expressed permission of the particular client manager)

During the presentation, I also ask some personal questions, such as, "Are you married? Do you have children? What are their ages?" I need to have this information so I know what to recommend. For example, I need to know approximately what an employee earns per hour so that I can help determine the appropriate policy that is affordable.

My approach is to help guide an employee to a policy with a reasonable deduction at each enrollment. This way, the employee gets used to the idea of having deductions, and in time may buy more coverage as his or her needs grow. To do this, I explain that the average deduction is about $10 per week. I might say, "Well, $10 is what most people are doing but you can do $7 or $8." This way, I am not pushing. I try to bring the client along gently without being too aggressive.

To interest a current insured to buy additional coverage, I might say, "It looks like your coverage may be light based on your needs and goals. You have $50,000 and that's good, but it may not be enough for your situation. You just had another baby, so you may need a little bit more." Depending on the situation, I may sell a term policy too. Another way I set the stage for increasing coverage is by comparing the employee's situation to mine. I might say, "According to insurance studies, most people have multiple policies within their lifetime. I must be average, because I have five." This approach softens the conversation and lets the employee know that I'm a consumer too. It also goes back to the "me too" idea.

I close with the rate sheet. I show the employee the appropriate modal deduction choices, and then ask, "What amount do you feel comfortable with on a weekly basis? Select something that's not going to change your lifestyle."

Rollovers and Cross-Selling

Not all sales originate from internal payroll-deducted policies. There are a lot of cross-selling opportunities within a re-enrollment that should be pursued. And when it comes to capturing business outside of the voluntary market, the interview worksheet is my strongest tool. As I review current coverage and take notes, I always ask, "Where did you work previously?" That specific question can open up a conversation that leads to a potential rollover situation. If employees have 401(k)s to roll over or other financial needs, I can try to earn that business too.

Recently, I asked a newly hired, 60-year-old grocery clerk, "Where did you work before coming here?" As we talked, she told me about her 401(k) plan from her previous employer. I made a note of this on her worksheet. The following year, during the annual voluntary benefit re-enrollment, we discussed her financial needs and timelines. As a result, she allowed me to roll over all $83,000 of her 401(k) into an annuity.

A worksite client in a grocery store's bakery department once called me for advice about his wife's old IRA account. We worked together to move some of their accounts into appropriate products outside of the employer's voluntary offering. That non-worksite sale resulted in a very satisfied client. A couple of weeks later, I received a call from the grocery manager at the same store who had just inherited $300,000 from his mother. He called me because of the recommendation he received from the employee in the bakery department. Within two weeks, he purchased a whole-life policy, and an annuity. It's a rare situation, but it's not the only one I have seen.

Service

I relieve the employer's human resources department of the service burden by explaining that I am the employees' point of service. With that role in mind, I have the information on file that is necessary to answer the questions or solve the problems.

I have created methods to address all types of service situations. For example, sometimes an employee will call me with a question, but forget to tell me the phone number where he or she can be reached. Or I might call an employee back and find that there is no way to leave a message. Instead of letting the request slip through the cracks, I mail a brochure or article that addresses the client's concern.

At times, employees simply don't understand their coverage or they might forget what they learned about the benefits of their policy and consider dropping it. Or, they may receive conflicting advice from another agent and call to cancel valuable coverage. Because I am their point of contact, I have the opportunity to personally address these concerns and misconceptions. Once we speak and they feel comfortable, they usually keep the policy. I make sure to visit with these folks during the next re-enrollment to cement their decision to keep their coverage. They appreciate the effort and good service experiences are often shared with other employees, which helps with policy persistency, maintains renewals and results in new sales, all important elements of a successful worksite business.

This old adage is true: "If you think it's easy to get a client, try to find a new one." There is a cost of acquiring a new worksite case, both in time and money. For larger cases, it typically takes 18 to 24 months to progress from the initial contact with the employer to the actual enrollment. That's a long time, but these valuable cases can be well worth the time it takes to get them in place. So, it only makes sense to take care of existing clients by re-enrolling and servicing them. I work my existing client base not just for their sake, but also for the sake of my business. What's more, when I take good care of my employer clients and their employees, I achieve my goal of helping others gain a measure of financial security. As enrollees become friends, they see that I believe in what I offer and that helps them feel good about their purchase. A re-enrollment is the action that says, "I believe in what I do."

Mark Petro has been an agent and a broker since 1987. He specializes in worksite marketing within retail environments with a heavy emphasis on re-enrollments. Because of his extensive knowledge of voluntary life insurance benefits and his outstanding policy persistency, he is a mentor to many of his fellow agents. In 2006, his main carrier asked him to teach sales trainers in Dallas, Texas, as well as assist with the company's selection of voluntary payroll-deducted products. Mark has been awarded the prestigious Ben Feldman Life Award of Excellence in 2003 and is a Qualifying member of the Million Dollar Round Table (1992 – 2007). In addition to achieving awards from his main carrier, he is also a multiple recipient of the National Association of Insurance and Financial Advisors (NAIFA) National Quality Award (1994 -2001), and NAIFA's National Sales Achievement Award (1992 -2001).

Mark Petro
President
Mark Petro and Associates
10333 Bartholomew Road
Auburn Twp., OH 44023
Phone: 440-543-3399
Fax: 440-543-3375
Email: mpetro@ft.newyorklife.com

Chapter Twenty-Six

Time Well Spent

PATRICIA J. REDIC

My father was a well-respected insurance professional for 36 years. He loved the business and believed in the power of life insurance. I grew up attending insurance-related events, stamping his brochures, listening as he memorized his presentations and reaping the rewards of his chosen profession. His diligence and dedication to the insurance industry paid for my braces, piano lessons, dozens of guinea pigs, a college education, a wedding and the down payment for my first home.

When my father learned he was dying of cancer, he asked me to join him and my brother in their insurance practice. That was the most important invitation of my life. I had but one brief year to work with him, and during that time, he introduced me to all of his clients. He specialized in high net worth individuals and large boardroom cases and told me to concentrate on those markets. As children often do, I immediately gravitated toward the opposite market. After he passed away, I discovered worksite marketing and immediately knew that this was the place for me.

My very first death claim delivery was to my mother. What a fitting way to begin my new career. It helped me understand the value and importance of insurance, and how it keeps families stable during times of sadness and need. Every day of my life is dedicated to what my father so strongly believed in.

When it first occurred to me to write a book about worksite marketing, I quickly realized that although I had more than 15 years of experience in the business, I surely didn't know enough about every facet to assume such a large task. So I decided to contact others in the business whom I respected. Each author was hand-selected as a result of reputation or referral and was asked to write about his or her area of expertise. Each wrote without knowing how the other contributing authors might present their views. No other parameters were given except for an approximate word count. This was done purposefully so that you, the reader, would see that there are many ways to approach worksite marketing, just as there are multiple ways to arrive at success within this market.

This book is a culmination of a year of combined effort. The contributing authors are not only the best and brightest in the industry, but they also are generous with their knowledge and experience, inspiring and, most of all, passionate. They gave their time, stories, motivation and expertise because they all share the common belief in what we do for a living. And they know that our industry will only become stronger by sharing their histories, ideas and experiences with others. These are the people I spent time with this past year. And I am much better off for that.

I encourage you to contact these contributing authors when you need help or advice. It will be time well spent for you too.

Afterword

Although this book provides methods and tips for worksite marketing processes, it more importantly offers a glimpse of each author's confidence in and commitment to this exciting business. They are living proof that offering voluntary benefits through worksite marketing can create successful and visible results for everyone involved. It is our sincere wish that you take what you have learned from this book and make the worksite marketing world better for you and all those you touch.

To order additional copies of this book, contact your favorite author or Millennium Star Publishing.

www.millenniumstarpublishing.com

Author Directory

Ronald Agypt
Senior Vice President
Combined Worksite Solutions, An Aon Company
1000 Milwaukee Avenue, 6th Floor
Glenview, IL 60025
Phone: 847-953-8003
Fax: 847-953-8266
Email: ronald.agypt@combined.com
Website: www.combinedworksite.com

Charles C. Baggs, FLMI, ACS
Executive Vice President and Chief Administrative Officer
Allstate Workplace Division
1776 American Heritage Life Drive
Jacksonville, FL 32224
Phone: 904-992-2613
Fax: 904-992-2939
Email: cbaggs@allstate.com
Website: www.allstateatwork.com

Christopher Bernardine Sr., CES
Managing Director
Employee Benefit Communications
2701 N Rocky Point Drive, Suite 220
Tampa, FL 33607
Phone: 813-639-0099
Fax: 813-639-0098
Email: chris.bernardine@ebcfl.com
Website: www.ebcfl.com

Susan C. Bianco, CLU
Benefit Enrollment Services, Inc.
8180 Brecksville Road, Suite 110
Cleveland, OH 44141
Phone: 440-838-1320
Fax: 440-838-8750
Email: sbianco@besibenefits.com
Website: www.besibenefits.com

Frank J. Dallago III
Director of Shared Services
Trion
2300 Renaissance Blvd.
King of Prussia, PA 19406
Phone: 610-945-1050
Fax: 610-945-1050
Email: fdallago@trion.com
Website: www.trion.com

Neiciee Durrence
Vice President, Voluntary Practice & Product Management
Unum
1 Fountain Square
Chattanooga, TN 37402
Phone: 423-294-7204
Fax: 423-294-1301
Email: ndurrence@unum.com
Website: www.unum.com

TJ Gibb
Senior Vice President, Marketing
KMG America Corporation
12600 Whitewater Drive
Minnetonka, MN 55343
Phone: 952-930-4806
Fax: 952-930-4802
Email: tj.gibb@kmgamerica.com
Website: www.humana.com

Carroll S. Golden
CLU, ChFC, CMFC, CLTC, LTCP, CASL, ALMI, ACS
Vice President Sales & Marketing
Transamerica Life Insurance Company
Long Term Care Division
1900 L. Don Dodson
Bedford, TX 76021
Phone: 817-285-3451
Cell: 817-709-6859
Fax: 817-285-3452
Email: cgolden@aegonusa.com

H. Chris Guckert
Managing Partner
Impact Enrollment Solutions
4500 Black Rock Road
Hampstead, MD 21074
Phone: 410-374-3958
Fax: 410-374-1306
Email: cguckert@impactenrollment.com
Website: www.impactenrollment.com

Robert L. Heston, Jr.
President and CEO
Legal Access Plans, L.L.C.
2401 Fountainview
Suite 300
Houston, TX 77057
Phone: 713-785-7400
Email: bheston@legalaccessplans.com
Website: www.legalaccessplans.com

Marion Holloway
Manager Client Relations
Vision Financial Corporation
17 Church Street
P.O. Box 506
Keene, NH 03431
Phone: 1-800-793-0223 ext. 206
Fax: 603-357-0250
Email: mholloway@visfin.com
Website: www.visfin.com

Marie J. Killian, J.D.
IHPM Practice Leader
Trion
2300 Renaissance Boulevard
King of Prussia, PA 19406
Business phone: 610-684-3270
Mobile phone: 610-420-8265
Email: mkillian@trion.com
Website: www.trion.com

Jason Krouse
Chief Marketing Officer
Cost Containment Group
1 Eileen Way
Syosset, NY 11791
Phone: 516-576-9264
Email: Jason@ccgfamily.com
Website: www.ccgfamily.com

Jordan K. Nadel
President
Falcon Technologies, Inc.
565 East Swedesford Road, Suite 218
Wayne, PA 19087
Voicemail: 610-977-7502
Fax: 610-977-7519
Email: jnadel@falctech.com
Website: www.falctech.com

Robert H. Noe
CEO
Millennium Benefits Group
46 Chagrin Plaza #103
Chagrin Falls, OH 44022
Phone: 440-286-2010
Fax: 440-286-2084
Email: mbg@mbenefitsgroup.com
Website: www.mbenefitsgroup.com

Louis J. Pantalone
Executive Vice President
Univers Workplace Benefits
897 12th Street
Hammonton, NJ 08037
Phone: 609-561-0240 Ext.4112
Fax: 610-537-9312
Email: Lou.Pantalone@Universworkplace.com
Website: www.universworkplace.com

Michael D. Perna
President and Founder
Voluntary Benefits Specialists, LLC
8766 S Maryland Parkway, Suite 105
Las Vegas, NV 89123
Phone: 702-533-4232
Fax: 702-837-5530
Email: MDP702@aol.com

Mark Petro
President
Mark Petro and Associates
10333 Bartholomew Road
Auburn Twp., OH 44023
Phone: 440-543-3399
Fax: 440-543-3375
Email: mpetro@ft.newyorklife.com

Jay Pettapiece
President
Vision Financial Corporation
17 Church Street
P.O. Box 506
Keene, NH 03431
Phone: 1-800-793-0223 ext. 207
Fax: 603-357-0250
Email: jpettapiece@visfin.com
Website: www.visfin.com

DC Redic
President
DC Redic, Consulting
dcredic@prodigy.net

Patricia J. Redic
President
Succeed With Style
46 Chagrin Plaza #103
Chagrin Falls, OH 44022
Phone: 440-286-2010
Fax: 440-286-2084
Email: pat@succeedwithstyle.com
Website: www.succeedwithstyle.com

Tony Roberts
A. Roberts & Associates, Inc.
13819 English Villa Drive
Louisville, KY 40245
Phone: 502-548-3065
Fax: 502-244-0420
Email: troberts@arobertsassociates.com
Website: www.Allstate.com/tonyroberts

Robert S. Shestack, CES
National Practice Leader: Voluntary Benefits
Trion
2300 Renaissance Boulevard
King of Prussia, PA 19406
Phone: 856-437-8555
Mobile: 856-278-5454
Fax: 856-437-8555
Email: rshestack@trion.com
Website: www.trion.com

Terry Tullo
President
New Benefits, Ltd
14240 Proton Road
Dallas, TX 75244
Phone: 800-800-8304 x1617
Fax: 972-201-0887
Email: ttullo@newbenefits.com
Website: www.newbenefits.com